MY SUMMERS ON HEMINGWAY ROAD

A Collection of Short Stories

By Alicia Hein Cook

Illustrations by Dave Lewis

Farmhouse Publishing

Printed in the United States of America

10 9 8 7 6 5 4 3

ISBN: 1484925823
ISBN-13: 978-1484925829

Cover illustration and design by Dave Lewis

This collection of short stories is based on the childhood memories of the author who spent her summers, while growing up, on Lake Charlevoix in Northern Michigan.

DEDICATION

To Mom & Dad, Grammy & Grand-dad for making my summers possible on Hemingway Road, and to the rest of my family and neighbors along my favorite road for making them joyous!

Hemingway Road

It was dirt and gravel,
the road we traveled,
to get to our favorite home.

The view of the lake,
boats making their wakes,
what a wonderful time in our lives.

The history of families,
three and four generations,
will remain in their summer abodes.

How I shall always,
treasure and cherish,
My summers on Hemingway Road.

- Alicia Hein Cook

Contents

For more information about the author and the book, please visit her official website, or send email to her:

Website:

www.hemingwayroad.com

Email:

Lishville@aol.com

The People of Hemingway Road...

(Birchmont)
Margaret Hemingway Bundy, Virginia Hemingway Spayde, and their husbands, Homer Bundy and George Spayde

Margaret and Virginia were first cousins to renowned author Ernest Hemingway. They were all good friends and neighbors. Margaret was particularly always cheerful and in good spirits.

(The Farmhouse)
The Brownlees

Robert, Adele, and their daughter, Bonnie. They lived in The Farmhouse, next door to Deck 'n Dock.

(Deck 'n Dock)
The Heins

Mom - Karel Shepard Hein. Mother of Alicia and Billy. She grew up on Hemingway Road during her summers in "Little Brown House."

Dad - G. William Hein. Father of Alicia and Billy. He and Mom built "Deck 'n Dock" in 1967, next door to Little Brown House.

Alicia Hein - The author. She was six years old in 1967.

Billy Hein - Older brother to Alicia. He was nine years old in 1967.

(Little Brown House)
The Shepards

Grammy – Alice Schroeder-Shepard. Maternal grandmother to Alicia, Billy, and "the cousins." She lived next to Deck 'n Dock in Little Brown House.

Uncle Jim - Jim Shepard. Karel Shepard's brother and uncle to Alicia and Billy. Father of the cousins.

Aunt Maxine - Maxine Shepard. Uncle Jim's wife and mother of the cousins. Jim, Maxine, and their children lived year-round in their home in Charlevoix on Lake Michigan.

(Little Brown House)
The Shepards
(continued)

"The Cousins"

Shelley Shepard - The oldest of Jim and Maxine Shepard's four children. She was nine years old in 1967 and a very good artist.

Scott Shepard - Seven years old in 1967 and a close companion to Billy.

Sheila Shepard - Five years old in 1967 and Alicia's partner in mischief.

Stephen Shepard - Three years old in 1967 and often left out because he was so young.

Tom Shepard - Karel and Jim's younger brother and uncle to Alicia, Billy, and "the cousins." Also known as U.T. (Uncle Tom)

The Kennedys   Bob, Louise, and their children Todd, Albie,
Louie, and David. They were from Dixon,
Illinois. David was a close companion to Alicia
and Billy. He was seven years old in 1967.

The Bulls   Ira and Thelma, an older couple from Lansing,
Michigan.

(MaHaSuBi)   Clarence ("Hargie") and Mabel, and their
The Hargraves   children Bill and Sue, who were grown up by
1967.

Harris Cabin   Edith Harris, a little old lady who lived in a log
cabin in the woods. She was very old and lived
primitively.

The Harknesses &   Dale, Joan, and their children Mike, Denise,
Newmans   and Barbie. Barbie was Alicia's age. Joan's
parents, the Harknesses, the children's
grandparents, spent their summers with them.

Annabelle Webb   A friend of Grammy's. Her daughter, Janet,
was grown and had a little girl, Jill, a few years

younger than Alicia.

The Harris Summer Home

At the very beginning of Hemingway Road was the original summer home of the entire Harris family (Edith's family). No one had lived there in many years. Edith's parents had long since passed away. Her sister, who was twenty years younger, Elizabeth Harris Aerne, lived in Charlevoix with her husband. The cottage was first in line on Hemingway Road. It was old and situated back into the trees. The yellowed white paint was peeling. Spider webs covered the outside of the old cottage. It reminded me of what a haunted house might look like. There was a big wagon wheel leaning against the side of the cottage.

Preface

Back in the early 1900s, a man named George Hemingway purchased a large amount of land in northern Michigan to start "The Hemingway Tree Farm." Some of the property was lake-front to Lake Charlevoix. George was the uncle of famous author Ernest Hemingway, who also spent his boyhood summers in northern Michigan. Oak Park, Illinois, had been the home of George and his family for many years until he moved with his wife, Anna, and his daughters, Virginia and Margaret, to Ironton, Michigan. They lived in "The Farmhouse," which was one of the cottages that was already there along the lakefront property. Since the dirt road had no name and they needed a mailing address, they decided to name it Hemingway Road. Later, George built a larger home for his family next door to The Farmhouse. It was given the name Birchmont, because it was surrounded by many wonderful white-barked birch trees. Along with the building of Birchmont, other summer cottages were being built on Hemingway Road.

Years later, my maternal grandparents, Mr. And Mrs. D. R. Shepard from Grand Rapids, Michigan, met a realtor in Charlevoix. His name was Earl Young. He showed my grandparents "Little Brown House," which wasn't so little, on Lake Charlevoix, in the small town of Ironton. The Wilsons owned *Little Brown House* at the time. My grandparents immediately fell in love with the cottage and purchased it for their family in 1948. My mother, Karel, was thirteen years old then. Her brother, Jim, was about eleven and their baby brother, Tom, was three. That is how my family became part of Hemingway Road.

I have been traveling down Hemingway Road for many years by car, bike, and by foot. The entrance to my favorite road was always a treasure to me! To leave the hot, black asphalt and enter the most welcoming of roads was always exciting!

As you turned onto the road, you were always reminded of friends and neighbors as each family who lived on Hemingway Road was listed on their very own sign. Two narrow logs were firmly planted into the ground about two feet apart. Several boards were hooked to each other with separate family names on each one. The boards were painted white with black lettering. Your sign was not hooked up unless you had arrived for the summer. When you left, your sign would be taken down. The first part of the road was in between trees and bushes. I always recalled the crabapple tree on the right side of the road. To the left you could hear chirping of crickets and locusts no matter what time of day, due to the fact this area was under four to six inches of water and was considered to be a marsh. Beyond the trees was the real treat! Lake Charlevoix was to the left. This view was most special on the first trip down Hemingway Road for the season! You would never see the same view twice. You may see a beautiful sailboat with a giant spinnaker blowing across the lake. All types of boats would be there at different times—Cabin Cruisers, row boats, speed boats, and all kinds of sailboats, along with pontoon boats. Once in a while, you would see a giant freighter coming to unload iron ore across the lake.

Further down Hemingway Road, there were other important landmarks. Around the bend from Annabelle Webb's cottage, there was a ditch to the right of the road that was a flowing stream. You could find minnows and little turtles in this stream. It ran all the way to Edith Harris' cottage. I rode my Stingray bike down Hemingway Road so many times during a summer that I had each rut memorized. You would also encounter several beautiful patches of Queen Anne's Lace, Daisies, and wild Gaillardia. This is my image of my beloved Hemingway Road.

At the very beginning of Hemingway Road, two logs painted white were buried into the ground. They held several small signs between them, bearing most of the aforementioned people who lived on Hemingway Road.

1 MY FIRST MEMORIES OF HEMINGWAY ROAD

My first memories of Hemingway Road are as clear as if I saw it for the first time yesterday. Actually, I was taken to Hemingway Road as an infant, but I was around four years old when I remember my first trip there.

Daddy worked for the Ann Arbor News in Ann Arbor, Michigan, where we lived. It was a very hot summer's day when we loaded up our station wagon and headed for Charlevoix and Hemingway Road. It was somewhere around 265 miles from Ann Arbor to Charlevoix, a good five and a half hour trip including stops for gas and dinner along the way. We were finally ready to go. Daddy, Mommy, Billy and I got into our white Dodge station wagon and were on our way to Grammy's Brown House on beautiful Lake Charlevoix and Hemingway Road. This was 1965 and air-conditioning in cars was not all that common yet. Our car, unfortunately, was not air-conditioned and the trip was hot and sticky, but well worth the trip to our lake! We stopped for dinner as it grew dark. After dinner, it was completely dark. Daddy said we had another hour and a half to go before we arrived at Grammy's. At least the hot sun had set and was not beating down on us; however, it was still hot and humid. I usually fell asleep on these trips, but I was too excited to sleep. I felt the car slowing down and heard the sound of our car on a dirt road. Without opening my eyes, I knew we were there! We were on Hemingway Road. I sat up to get my first glance at Lake Charlevoix. I could see the lights around the shoreline reflecting off the lake. It looked like glass, it was so calm. After passing several cottages, we turned up the steep hill that led to the last few cottages on Hemingway Road. Daddy pulled into Grammy's driveway where a big brown garage stood and next to it a long brown shed used for storage on one side and extra sleeping quarters on the other side. When my mother was a teenager, she used to use the sleeping quarters end of the shed. She fixed it all up and used it as her own little "get-away" place. Grammy heard us pull in and came up the back hill from *Little Brown House* to greet us. Daddy unloaded the car while Grammy got out some refreshments she had baked and some nice cold lemonade, too. After our refreshments, we talked for a while then Daddy asked, "Who would like a cool dip in the lake?" Billy and I rose to the occasion and got ready. All of us went in except Grammy, who came to sit on the beach and watch us. How calm and cool the lake was! I could not swim yet, but Daddy held me afloat while Mommy and Billy splashed about. What a way to relax after a steamy five and a half hour trip!

The mornings could sometimes be pretty nippy. I remember getting dressed in a hurry so as not to freeze, and then going downstairs to the kitchen. There are three doors to the kitchen. One leads out to the screened porch across the front, one leads out to a little back room with a big laundry tub sink, a bathroom with a door leading to the back yard. The remaining door leads into the living room. This door was always kept closed in the mornings, to keep the heat from the black pot-belly stove trapped in the kitchen. It felt so warm and cozy in the cheery *Little Brown House* kitchen. The smell of bacon, eggs, and coffee permeated throughout the cottage. It would usually warm up outside by 10:00 a.m. I was anxiously awaiting the arrival of my cousins. They lived in Grand Rapids, Michigan. We were all spending the Fourth of July holiday together. There was Uncle Jim, Aunt Maxine, Shelley, Scott, Sheila, and Stephen. I was waiting outside on the back porch when Uncle Jim's station wagon pulled in next to ours. As I ran up the stairs in the back yard, car doors were flying open. I hugged Sheila and then everyone else. Mom, Dad, Grammy, and Billy all came out to say, "Hello!" As they brought their belongings in, *Little Brown House* became very full for the next week. We would visit *Little Brown House* periodically throughout the summer months. We found out that Aunt Maxine and Uncle Jim and the cousins would be moving to Charlevoix permanently. A few months later, my parents had some news of their own concerning our future summers on Hemingway Road.

2 CHRISTMAS IN CHARLEVOIX

We were used to hot weather and cool off-shore breezes during our summers on Hemingway Road, but winters were quite another thing. Michigan is known for its harsh winters, especially Northern Michigan where Charlevoix is situated. We were anxiously awaiting Dad's arrival home from work so that we could begin our five and a half hour trip up to Uncle Jim's and the cousins'. We were going to Charlevoix for Christmas. We would be staying with the cousins in Charlevoix for Christmas and then checking on the progress of our new cottage being built next to *Little Brown*

House on Hemingway Road. We could not stay on Hemingway Road as it was snowed in and desolate during the winter months. Mom was packing the station wagon with warm clothes and Christmas presents. Grammy was already in Charlevoix. I couldn't wait to see her! I was standing at our front door when I saw Dad driving up in his Mustang. "Mom! Mom! Dad's home, we can go now!" We all got into the station wagon bound for Christmas in Charlevoix. The trip this time was so different! We went the same way as always, through Lansing, St. John, Mt. Pleasant, Gaylord, Elmira, Boyne Falls, and Boyne City.

When we traveled in the spring and summer, it was such a different sight; flowers and trees blooming. Now, snow grew deeper and deeper the farther north we drove. Everything was in a blanket of white snow! Even though the trip seemed long, I was so excited to visit and spend the holidays with my cousins! We finally arrived in Boyne City. Dad called Aunt Maxine from a pay phone in the Dairy Queen parking lot. How different it looked all boarded up.

"Well, Max, we'll be there in about thirty minutes."

"Great, the stew pot is on."

"We'll see you then," said Dad.

Even though I hated stew, I was happy to see my cousins! When we arrived at Uncle Jim's house on Michigan Avenue, it was evident that winter was upon us! I was used to sand and sun in Charlevoix; now, I saw snow and sleet. As we walked into the cousins' house, I saw a beautiful tree lit up in big colored lights. We sat down for dinner. The kids' table had a view overlooking Lake Michigan, half frozen. It looked so different during the summer. Uncle Jim and Aunt Maxine lived on Michigan Avenue in an old, English, Tudor-style house on Lake Michigan. It had two staircases, one in the front hall, and a green spiral staircase leading down to the kitchen. After dinner, we went to the basement to play. Our moms and dads and Grammy were having coffee in the living room. Meanwhile, we were playing various games in the basement. We girls were playing house and serving dinner with play dishes. The boys, however, had gotten a red Greyhound wagon out and were pushing little Stephen around, cutting sharp curves about one hundred miles per hour.

"You boys better stop that!" screamed Shelley. "You're going to make Stephen crash!"

All of a sudden, the wagon with Stephen rolled over. Stephen, who was only two, was screaming loud as a siren. Shelley ran over and picked him up off the cement floor.

"He's okay!" said Shelley. "He just has a lump on his forehead."

Just then, we heard Uncle Jim coming down the stairs.

"What happened?" He walked over to Shelley and picked up Stephen. "Are you okay, little guy?" When he saw that Stephen was okay, he put him down. "What happened?"

"We were giving Stephen a ride in the wagon and he fell off," said Scott.

"Maybe you guys were going just a little too fast with this little fellow!" exclaimed Uncle Jim. He then picked up the red wagon and put it in the woodshed. "This is an outdoor toy!" He said.

We were all quite as church mice as Uncle Jim climbed back up the basement stairs. When he reached the top and closed the door, we all began to giggle.

"You boys always do dumb stuff!" said Shelley.

"Aw, be quiet!" said Scott.

I noticed all the sleds and a toboggan against the wall. "Let's go sledding," I said.

"In the dark, you nut?" asked Billy.

"We can go sledding tomorrow," replied Shelley.

"The hill down to the beach is all iced over and really fast!" said Scott.

"C'mon kids!" yelled down Aunt Maxine. "It's time for bed."

"Okay, Mom," answered Shelley.

We all marched up two flights of stairs to bed.

I loved Shelley and Sheila's room. It had twin beds, pink walls, and red carpet. There was a cot for me to sleep on. The boys were down the hall with bunk beds and a cot for Billy.

"Let's spy on the boys," said Sheila.

"Yeah, let's!" I answered.

Shelley agreed unanimously.

The three of us crept down the hallway. I could feel the cool of Northern Michigan upon my bare toes. We peeked around the corner of their room and then we pulled back and held our hands over our mouths so we wouldn't laugh out loud. We did it again and then giggled. The next time, we leaned in toward the door and there were the boys.

"BOO!" They said.

"EEK!" We screamed and ran back to our room with the boys chasing us.

"You girls go to sleep!" said Aunt Maxine.

So, we did!

The next day was Christmas Eve Day. We had breakfast and got all bundled up in our snowsuits to go sledding. Sheila and I were the last ones to get ready. The other kids had already gone.

"Hey," I said. "There are no sleds left; they took all of them."

Sheila looked all around the basement. "I know!" She exclaimed. "We can use that blue plastic boat."

"That's for swimming," I said.

"What's the difference if it's used on water or snow?" asked Sheila.

"I guess you're right!" I said.

So, off we went out of the basement door, each carrying an end of the blue plastic boat. When we got to the hill down to the beach, we saw Billy, Scott and Shelley at the bottom. We put the boat level, so we could both get into it.

"What are you two crazies doing?" asked Billy.

All their mouths opened wide as we shoved off and hung onto each side of our "land yacht"! Boy, did we fly! I could almost feel the ice coming through the bottom of the boat. What a rough ride! We were going so fast that Billy and Shelley could not stop us, but managed to slow us down some. We went a little farther and then hit a bump and spun around. We then came to a stop. Billy, Shelley and Scott ran over to us.

"Boy, you two looked really stupid sledding down the hill in a boat!" said Scott.

"Yeah," laughed Billy.

"I'm just glad they're alright!" said Shelley. "It's hard work keeping all of you alive. Look! There are holes in the bottom of the boat from the rough trip down the hill."

"Now it will sink next summer," grumbled Scott.

"My feet are cold. I want to go home," I complained.

"Me too," said Sheila.

"You babies go home and we'll be back in an hour," said Scott.

When we got home, Grammy was in the kitchen making lunch.

"We're cold, Grammy!" I said.

"Well, I have some hot chicken noodle soup for you. Are you girls excited about Christmas?" asked Grammy.

"Oh, yes!" we exclaimed.

After lunch, we helped Grammy make cut-out sugar cookies. Our parents went out to lunch. We made sugar cookies in the shape of bells, stars, Santas, Christmas trees, and camels. It was around 4:00 p.m.

"Girls," said Grammy. "You two go take a bath and put on your jammies. That way, the other children can take one when they get back. Be quiet, though. Stephen is taking a nap."

"Okay," we agreed.

"I'm going to start Christmas Eve dinner."

We went upstairs. It was a cold and drafty day. You could hear the wind howling outside the house. We made a deep, hot bubble bath.

"What do you want for Christmas?" asked Sheila.

"I want an easy-bake oven! What do you want, Sheila?" I asked.

"I want Mouse Trap, Barrel of Monkeys, and lots of toys!"

"Yeah, lots of toys!" I yelled.

After our baths, we put on our warm flannel jammies and our blue fuzzy robes that Grammy had given us last year.

When we came downstairs it was dark outside. Our parents were in the living room having cocktails, cheese, and crackers. The Christmas tree was especially beautiful tonight, almost as if it knew it was Christmas Eve.

"Dinner's ready," said Grammy.

We went into the dining room to the kids' table. Beautiful china and crystal glasses decorated the table. We had roast beef, twice-baked potatoes, peas and carrots, Jell-O with bananas, whipped cream, and dinner rolls. We had a great dinner!

After dinner, Grammy put out trays of cookies, homemade fudge, and eggnog. As Christmas music played in the background, we visited and laughed for about an hour.

"Okay, kids," said Aunt Maxine. "It's time to hang your stockings and go to bed."

So, we hung our stockings with care and scooted off to bed. Mommy came up to tuck us all into bed. She came to each of us, gave us a kiss, and said, "I'll see you on Christmas! Sweet dreams!"

I was so excited, I couldn't sleep. "I wish it was morning already!" said Sheila.

"Me too!" said Shelley.

"Me three!" I said. "You want to spy on the boys again?" I asked.

"No!" said Sheila. "Santa won't come if we aren't asleep!"

"Oh, yeah!" I exclaimed. "You're right."

We all fell asleep, but later that night, I awakened with a terrible leg cramp. I wanted to go to Mommy and Daddy, but I was afraid Santa would catch me out of bed and not leave any presents. My leg hurt so badly that I finally got up the nerve and went to my parents' room.

"What's the matter, Lishie?" asked Mommy.

"My leg hurts a lot!"

"I'll bet you have a Charlie horse," said Daddy.

Mommy gave me some children's aspirin and tucked me back into bed. I fell fast asleep.

The next thing I knew, Shelley and Sheila were tapping me.

"Get up, Lishie! It's Christmas morning!" said Shelley.

"It's still dark out," I said, rubbing my eyes.

Then the boys came running into our room. "Merry Christmas!" they yelled at the top of their lungs.

Aunt Maxine, Mommy, and Grammy were waiting at the top of the stairs so we wouldn't go down. It was a long-time family tradition to wait for the men to build a fire in the fireplace, put on Christmas music, and ring the special Christmas bells. We stood around the top of the stairs. Little baby Stephen was saying "Merry Christmas!"

Finally, the Christmas bells rang. "Hooray!" We all started running down the stairs. Everyone was saying "Merry Christmas!"

Oh Come All Ye Faithful was playing on the stereo. Daddy picked me up and kissed me. "Merry Christmas," he said. He lifted down my stocking for me. The noise of ripping paper was loud! Little Stephen got a "top" that spun around when you pushed down the handle. It had a scene inside it. I got mittens, Tinkerbell perfume, and colored bubble bath powders. I got chocolate Santas, silly putty, new slippers, and all three of us girls got a beautiful Raggedy Ann necklace with moveable arms and legs. We got peppermint candy canes and a huge plastic candy cane full of candy.

After we opened our stockings, we had the best breakfast ever! Scrambled eggs, bacon, sausage, sweet rolls, orange juice, and fruit were served.

After breakfast, we got dressed in our new Christmas outfits. We still had all of our tree presents to open. We were all in the family room playing with the presents we got when we heard the doorbell ring. Uncle Jim answered it.

"Hi Tom!" answered Uncle Jim.

"Merry Christmas, everyone!" answered Uncle Tom.

We all rushed up to him and gave him hugs and kisses. He had two shopping bags full of presents. Uncle Tom attended Ferris State College. He put his presents for everyone under the tree and then sat in a chair. Shelley went to sit on his lap.

We were all waiting patiently to open our gifts. Finally, all our parents came into the living room. Aunt Maxine was going to hand out the presents. After a few minutes, everyone was ooh-ing and aw-ing. Grammy and Aunt Maxine both got a mink stole. I got the "easy bake oven" I desperately wanted! Sheila got "Mouse Trap." We were all getting what we wanted. After the last gift was opened, it was time for Christmas dinner: Baked ham, turkey, stuffing, sweet potatoes, corn, and green beans. We had all kinds of cookies and cakes for dessert. What a wonderful Christmas all of us had! One I would remember forever!

3 THE PROGRESS OF DECK 'N DOCK

Christmas had passed, but we still had a week left in Charlevoix. We drove into Ironton, pulling Uncle Jim's snowmobiles behind us on a trailer. We took` a picnic of hotdogs, baked beans, and potato salad. We were going to roast them in *Little Brown House's* fireplace. Our cottage was in the process of being built. We were going to check on how far along the builders had gotten. As we drove down the hill into Ironton, I spotted the Ironton ferry tied up and shut down. It was very odd to see it like that. I was used to seeing it in full operation during the summer.

Uncle Jim and Daddy got the snowmobiles off the trailer. Uncle Jim hooked up a special sled behind one of the snowmobiles. First, they took Mom, Dad, Bill, Scott, and Stephen across the very frozen Lake Charlevoix. Grammy stayed behind with Shelley, Sheila, and me. About fifteen minutes later, Aunt Maxine came back for us. Grammy rode on the snowmobile with Aunt Maxine. Shelley, Sheila, and I rode in the sled behind them. It was fun riding across the lake in a snowmobile sled instead of a boat.

Half way across the lake, the sled became unhitched. It must not have been clamped down all the way. Aunt Maxine and Grammy kept going.

"Mom will notice soon that she lost us," said Shelley. They were almost across the lake when Aunt Maxine looked back and noticed our sled was missing.

"Thank goodness she turned around. We look kind of dumb just sitting in a sled in the middle of a frozen lake," replied Shelley. Sheila and I both laughed.

"What are you girls doing out here?" laughed Aunt Maxine.

"Ice fishing," giggled Sheila.

"Okay, we're all set now!" said Aunt Maxine.

When we got to Hemingway Road, we helped carry the picnic into *Little Brown House.* Then we went over to look at how far along the builders were. It looked very big inside! The view from the upper level was great! I could see ice shanties all over the frozen lake. I closed my eyes and imagined what the view would be like with boats all over the lake, sunshine and trees. I couldn't wait for our first summer in our new cottage!

We went back to *Little Brown House* for our picnic. *Little Brown House* was always bright and cheery in the summer. The sun would shine right through the wicker furniture on the porch. It was now dark and dreary because there were wood blinds up on all of the windows.

Grammy pulled away the big fireplace screen and let us throw the colored sprinkles into the fire. She then replaced the screen. The sprinkles made the flames look as colorful as a rainbow.

"Can we go outside now?" asked Scott.

"Stay in front of the cottages so we can see you," said Uncle Jim.

"Okay," we all shouted.

We started to gear up for the deep snow. We all walked down toward the lake. It was frozen solid.

"Hey! Look at me!" said Billy. "I'm out over my head, standing over the first rock pile."

We all ventured out on frozen Lake Charlevoix in our heavy snowsuits. After sliding around on the ice and a great snowball fight, we were ready to go home.

Next time we came to Hemingway Road, our new cottage would be ready for its first summer. We enjoyed another few days with the cousins then returned to Ypsilanti, where my daddy was now the manager of the Ypsilanti Press. What a great holiday season we had. There would be more memories to make in the years to come. Goodbye, Hemingway Road, until next June.

4 DECK 'N DOCK IS FINISHED!

After several years of staying at *Little Brown House*, Mom and Dad decided it was time to build a summer home of their own as it could get very crowded over at *Little Brown House* at times. There was a vacant lot next to *Little Brown House*, so Mom and Dad built the first year-round summer home on Hemingway Road. It was the "upside-down house," with the living room, dining room, and kitchen on the second floor and the three bedrooms downstairs. It was a two-story, split-level with eight sliding glass doors, three across the front of the cottage, two on the other side, and three across the front on the lower level. There was a big deck that went all the way around the cottage's second level. The view of the lake from the deck was breathtaking! Mom would furnish the deck with redwood furniture and two big umbrellas that would be visible from the other side of the lake. Each bedroom had its own sliding panel door leading out to a long concrete patio, followed by steps and a path leading to the lake.

We were all set with our very own summer home with a deck and a beach and a dock, which is how our favorite home got its name. Deck 'n Dock was ready the summer of 1967 for many seasons of summer fun! Thank you, Mom and Dad, for building Deck 'n Dock.

5 PREPARING FOR DECK 'N DOCK'S FIRST SUMMER

It was springtime, 1967, and the snow from winter was gone for good. I was almost six years old and Billy was almost nine. Billy and I still attended St. Paul's Lutheran School in Ann Arbor, Michigan. Daddy drove us in the mornings and Mommy picked us up in the afternoons. It was around a half an hour's trip from our house to school one way.

One Thursday afternoon, when Mommy picked us up from school, she announced we would be going up to Hemingway Road for the weekend to start moving into Deck 'n Dock. We were excited about our weekend at Deck 'n Dock and could hardly wait!

"Kids, come downstairs for dinner," said Dad. "I spoke with both the phone and power companies, so we have both working electricity and a telephone when we arrive."

"Wonderful!" said Mommy. "It would be a worthless trip if we didn't have any power up there to clean up the place!"

The next day, Billy and I went off to school. "Daddy," I said. "Are we leaving after dinner tonight?"

"No, I am getting off work early. Mommy and I will pick you up after school and we'll leave for Deck 'n Dock from there."

"Oh, good!" I exclaimed.

"You two have a good day in school!"

"Bye Daddy!"

"Bye kids. See you this afternoon," said Daddy.

School seemed to take longer than usual! Finally, 3:00 p.m. rolled around. Mommy and Daddy were sitting in our red Ford station wagon that we had gotten a few months before. The back part of the station wagon was packed full with things for Deck 'n Dock.

"How was school?" asked Daddy.

"Fine," I said. "But the lunch was yucky! My teacher made me eat everything."

"That won't kill you. It's good for you," said Mommy.

Within ten minutes, we were entering the expressway.

"We'll get a good two-hour head start on the Friday night traffic since we're leaving early," said Daddy.

"Daddy?"

"Yes, Alicia?"

"How far is Mt. Pleasant from Hemingway Road?"

"It's the exact half-way mark," said Daddy. "We'll stop at the Holiday Inn at Mt. Pleasant for dinner."

"Is that the place with the lobsters?" I asked.

"Yes, Sister-bell," said Daddy.

"Goody, I like to watch them!"

"All they are is giant crayfish," said Billy.

"Billy, let's catch some crayfish this weekend, okay?"

"Okay. I'll make some crayfish poles. Dad, you can use the ones we catch

17

for bait," said Billy.

"I'd love to, Billy, but I don't think I'll have time for fishing this weekend. We're going to be very busy getting Deck 'n Dock ready."

"Mommy, I'm bored."

"Well, Alicia, I have a little surprise for you and your brother," said Mommy. She handed us each a drawstring cloth bag she had made. Long white shoelaces were the handles. Billy's was red and blue plaid and mine was solid red. Inside my bag, I found a
"Little Kiddle Doll" with a car, some little books, and a troll doll, a pad of paper, and a box of crayons.

"Wow! Thanks, Mommy!"

"Yeah, thanks!" added Billy.

"You're welcome," said Mommy.

Inside Billy's bag there was a deck of playing cards, some books, some pens and paper, and a little magnetic checker game. Billy started reading and I played with my new little doll and car.

"Hey Lish? Do you want to play cards?"

"Okay, what game?"

"How about War?"

"Okay, that's a fun game."

"Billy, you don't have to shuffle the cards for so long!"

"Yes I do. It's a brand new deck."

"Don't start arguing before you start the game," warned Daddy.

"Okay, we won't," we replied.

"Bill, when we get there, we'll unload the bed linens and blankets and get the beds made up," said Mommy.

"That sounds like a good idea," said Daddy. "I'm glad we set up the bed frames the last time we were there. That will save a lot of time."

"I'm going to have the kids both sleep in Alicia's room tonight. There are twin beds in there. That way, we can work on finishing Billy's room with the bunk beds and my mother has a dresser at *Little Brown House* that we can have."

"Sounds good to me," said Daddy.

"I'm not going to play anymore!"

"Hey, hey, hey!" exclaimed Daddy. "You pick up those cards, Alicia Louise!"

"Well, Billy's cheating!"

"I am not! She's mad because I'm winning!"

"Well," said Mommy. "Put the cards away."

"Ouch, she's kicking me."

"Alicia, behave!" said Daddy.

Mommy turned around and drew an imaginary line down the middle of the back seat and told us both to stay on our own side. Billy resumed reading and I was still mad at him for winning, so I took my index finger and touched over the line.

"Mom, she's touching my side!"

"Alicia, you're asking for trouble. Now, behave!" said Mommy. "We're pulling off on the next exit for dinner."

"Good, I'm hungry!" said Billy.

"Me too!" I said.

The Holiday Inn in Mt. Pleasant was right off the highway. We stopped there quite often, unless we made it all of the way to Gaylord's Holiday Inn. I loved looking in the big lobster tank while we were waiting for our dinner.

I ordered my usual fried chicken, mashed potatoes, and chocolate milk.

"Alicia, can't you finish your dinner?"

"No, I'm too full!"

"You've only eaten a few bites."

"She ate too many crackers before dinner came," said Daddy.

Soon, we were on our way again. It started to get dark and I fell asleep.

When I woke up, we were there.

"Well, here we are in our new cottage," said Daddy.

The only furniture we had were the beds in the bedrooms. Deck 'n Dock's bedrooms were on the lower level. Mine was first, and then Billy's, and then Mommy's and Daddy's. Each of our bedrooms had their own sliding glass doors with a beautiful view of Lake Charlevoix.

Daddy unloaded the car, brought in a portable black and white television, and set it up for Billy and me to watch.

"Dad?" asked Billy. "Can we go down to the lake?"

"No, it's too dark. You can see everything in the morning."

"Okay," said Billy.

Since it was early in the spring, no one else was on Hemingway Road. All of the other cottages still had their winter blinds up. *Little Brown House* looked sad because it was also boarded up and Grammy was not there. Most people arrived and opened their cottages mid-June. This was only the beginning of May.

Mommy went to use the hot water, only to discover there wasn't any.

"Bill!" yelled Mommy.

"Yes, Dear," replied Daddy.

"There is no hot water."

"Let me check the circuit breaker," said Daddy.

"Okay," said Mommy.

"Does it work now?" asked Daddy.

"No!" replied Mommy.

We waited an hour and then Daddy figured out that the builder had forgotten to hook up some wires. Mommy called Uncle Jim in Charlevoix and told him we had no hot water until tomorrow when we could have it fixed.

"If you don't mind the ride into town, you could come here for showers, plus we could visit for a while."

"You talked us into it!" Mommy accepted.

So, we got back into the car and went to Uncle Jim and Aunt Maxine's. When we got there, I was very disappointed because my cousins were already asleep. Our parents visited over coffee for a while until Daddy said we should leave before the ferry closes for the night. We said "Good bye" and headed back for Hemingway Road.

"Okay, kids," said Mommy. "Your beds are all made up and it's time for bed."

I could hear Mommy and Daddy busily working upstairs, putting dishes into the cupboards and unpacking boxes.

The next morning, we ate breakfast and headed out the door to say hello to the lake.

"Stay close, kids. We're going to town shortly."

"Okay Dad."

We went down to the beach and felt the water. It was freezing! It usually wouldn't warm up until July. The lake was quiet; there were not any boats around. There would not be until Memorial Day weekend.

I could hear the ferry making a trip across the lake. "Come on, kids. We're going to town, now."

We ran up the hill to the car and we were soon on our way to Charlevoix.

"I'm glad we're going to Charlevoix instead of Boyne City!"

"Why, Alicia?" asked Mommy.

"Because," I said. "We get to ride on the ferry."

We pulled up to the ferry's gates. The ferry was on the other side of the lake, so we would have to wait about five minutes. It cost thirty-five cents to cross the lake on the ferry. Daddy paid Turk, the ferry operator.

"Daddy? May I have the orange ticket?"

"Sure you can," Daddy answered.

"Bill, we'll have to get a book of tickets on our way back from town since we'll be using the ferry a lot," said Mommy.

"We'll get them on the way back," replied Daddy.

Turk pulled down the big iron gates and Daddy drove off of the ferry and up a big hill to a stop sign. He turned right and we were off to Charlevoix. It was about a five minute trip. When we got to town, Daddy pulled into Oleson's Shopping Center. First, we went into the Variety store and then we went into the grocery store.

After we finished shopping, we returned to Hemingway Road. Mommy and Daddy told us to keep out of their way because they would be busy!

I was watching television when I noticed Billy throwing rocks into a pile by the shoreline.

"Mommy?"

"What, Alicia?"

"Billy is wading in the lake!"

"Yes, he asked and I told him that he could."

"May I?"

"As long as you don't get your clothes wet!"

"I won't!"

"Billy, what are you doing?"

"I'm building a little walkway out into the lake."

"Can I help?"

"Sure. Just throw medium-sized rocks onto the middle part of the pile."

"Okay."

"See? I've got the walkway part done."

"Now, I'll help you with the main pile."

"Billy, I'm tired of doing this!"

"Okay. You can sit and watch. It's almost done, anyway."

"It sure is strange here when nobody else is here yet!"

"Well, it will only be a few weeks more and then everyone will be coming up," said Billy. "There! It's finished," said Billy, proudly.

"Boy, this is really neat, Billy."

"You can walk out onto the water without getting wet. I'm going to call it Little Rock Island," said Billy.

"Kids, time for dinner!" called Daddy.

"We'll be right up!" we answered.

"Yum, pizza is my favorite!"

"Billy and I made a little rock island."

"You did?" asked Mommy.

"We'll take a look at it after dinner," said Daddy.

As Mommy cleared off the table, she let out a big sigh. "You kids will have to learn to wipe your feet! There is sand everywhere from your shoes. Keep the sand on the beach!"

"Okay, we get the picture," said Billy.

The next day was here, already. Daddy put our suitcases into the station wagon. We would be leaving to return to Ypsilanti shortly. I was sure we'd be on our way back up to Deck 'n Dock for the whole summer very soon!

6 SETTLING IN FOR OUR FIRST SUMMER

School was out for the summer and Mommy spent her days packing us up for the entire summer on Hemingway Road. Daddy will spend the weekends with us and travel back and forth to Ypsilanti. For this reason, Daddy drove his car and Mommy drove the station wagon to Charlevoix. That way, Daddy went home during the week and Mommy still had a car to use.

It was the morning of June 18, 1967; both cars were packed and we were ready to head to Deck 'n Dock for the entire summer. Billy rode with Mommy and I rode with Daddy in the Mustang. I called that car "the horsey" because the emblem was a Mustang horse.

"Is the house locked up?"

"Yes, Karel," said Daddy.

"Well, we're all ready," replied Mommy. "Billy and I will follow you and Alicia."

"Okay," said Daddy.

"Daddy, I love riding with you!"

"We have a lot of fun together, don't we?" answered Daddy.

Daddy turned on the radio and we sang along to it.

Mommy and Billy were right behind us.

"I think we'll stop here at the next exit for lunch," said Daddy.

"Oh, good!" I replied.

As we pulled off onto the exit ramp, I turned around to see if Mommy and Billy turned off, and they did.

After lunch, we were on our way again. We only had two more hours to go. The trip always seemed shorter when I traveled with Daddy because I had so much fun with him! It was a lot better than having Billy pick on me all the way. Daddy and I talked and played guessing games. Before I knew it, we were in the town where they had pictures of swans hanging off the lamp posts. The name of the little town was East Jordan, home of the East Jordan Ironworks.

"We'll be at the cottage in about 25 minutes," said Daddy.

"I can't wait! Grammy will be there and a lot of our neighbors, too!" I said. "Daddy, do you have to go back home soon?"

"No, I have a two-week vacation starting Monday. Then, I have another two weeks later on in the summer," said Daddy.

"Oh, I'm so glad," I said.

"Well, here we are," said Daddy as we turned off of Ferry Road onto Hemingway Road.

Lake Charlevoix was calm and so very beautiful as we drove down our favorite road.

"Look Daddy, Mrs. Webb is here."

Daddy stopped in front of Annabelle Webb's beach.

"Hello, Bill and Alicia!"

"Hello Annabelle!" said Daddy.

"Are you up for the summer now?" asked Mrs. Webb.

"Yes, we are," answered Daddy. "We'll get together soon!"

"Nice to have seen you," said Mrs. Webb.

Daddy and I drove on. Mommy and Billy stopped to talk to Mrs. Webb, too. As we drove further on down the road, we noticed several cottages had been opened and our friends were up on Hemingway Road for the summer.

"First thing we do is start unloading the cars," said Daddy.

"Oh, Daddy, I hate doing that!"

"Well, how can we do anything if we leave all our clothes in the car?" asked Daddy.

"Oh, alright," I mumbled.

Just then, Mommy and Billy drove in beside us. We carried endless loads of suitcases, boxes, and bags. I thought it would never end, but by 5:00 p.m., we were all unloaded.

"You kids were such good workers; I am going to take all of you to the Dairy Queen in Boyne City for dinner."

"Alicia, go next door to *Little Brown House* and invite Grammy.

"Okay!" I ran next door and Grammy was glad to accept our invitation.

Boyne City was about a twenty-minute trip from Hemingway Road. We did not have to ride the Ironton Ferry to get to Boyne City. It was a very scenic drive; half of the trip was lakefront.

"Kids, you can come with me to order and help carry the food back to the car," said Daddy.

Grammy and Mommy had found a picnic table by a little stream. Next door to the Dairy Queen was Don's Barber Shop. There was a giant pair of scissors painted on the side of his building.

"After we finish eating, we must go to the grocery store!" said Mommy.

"Oh, good, I need to pick up some things, too," said Grammy.

"We need a lot more than a few things!" said Mommy.

A few minutes later, we were at the A&P Grocery Store. Mommy's cart was filled to the top when she checked out. When we returned to Hemingway Road, it was dark. We all helped carry the groceries inside. Grammy, Mommy, and Daddy all had coffee while Billy and I rummaged through the goodies Mommy bought. Pretty soon, it was time for bed.

The next morning was bright and beautiful.

"We're not going anywhere today. We're just going to settle in and relax," said Daddy.

"Look, Daddy. There's Grammy out in her yard," I said.

"Alice? Come on up for some coffee."

"Thanks, Bill. I'll be right up."

Just then, Mommy came up from the downstairs bedrooms. Who were you yelling at, Bill?" asked Mommy.

"I was inviting your mother up for some coffee."

"Oh, great!" said Mommy.

"Some men are coming out here later to put up our dock. I want you kids to stay out of their way so you won't get hurt," said Daddy.

"We will," answered Billy.

About a half an hour later, a red jeep with a flashing light, pulling a trailer, pulled in front of our beach. The jeep read "Bay Marine."

Daddy came out of Deck 'n Dock and down the hill. He spoke to a very short man who must have been the owner. Two other men started carrying sections of dock down to the water. Billy and I sat on the beach and watched the men put up the dock. Now we could go fishing and cast our poles right out to the rock piles.

A lot of boats would come and anchor there because the fish liked to live in the rock piles. There were rock pile one, two, and three. The rock piles were left behind from a huge piling dock that was built around 1910 for the lumber boats that picked up cut lumber long ago. The dock was long gone, but the rock piles remained under water.

After the men were finished, Daddy gave the short man a check and they all left. Daddy walked onto the dock with us. Daddy told us that it was five feet deep at the end of the dock and that it was over my head, so to be careful not to fall in.

"Bill, kids, it's time for lunch."

"Okay, we're coming," Daddy hollered back.

"Well, Karel, how does the dock look from up here?" Daddy asked.

"That's just fine. But, more importantly, how sturdy is it?"

"As sturdy as a dock can be," answered Daddy.

"You kids are going to stay with Grammy this afternoon while Daddy and I go into town to look at some furniture for our deck. We'll be back in time for dinner, so don't you kids get into any mischief while we're away!" said Mommy.

"We won't," we both answered.

Billy and I went down to the beach. Grammy came down after about twenty minutes.

"Grammy?" asked Billy. "Can we all go out for a row boat ride?"

"I don't see why not," said Grammy.

"Billy, go up to the cabin in back where we keep the life jackets and get three of them. Get a smaller one for Lishie," said Grammy.

We put our life jackets on while Grammy just held hers across her lap.

"Get into the back, Lish," said Billy.

Grammy and Billy pushed the row boat off the beach and almost into the water.

"Now, you get in, Billy, and then I'll get in last," said Grammy.

Billy rowed the long wooden oars. They made a loud squeaky noise as if they needed to be oiled. I liked to watch the little whirlpool each stroke made in the water. The water was calm this afternoon and you could see the bottom of the lake very clearly. We rode over the rock piles and could see a few schools of fish.

"What a pleasant ride, Billy," said Grammy.

"Let's go in, now," said Billy. "My arms are getting tired."

When we got back, Grammy and Billy got out and pulled the little row boat up by a rope. I was still seated in the boat, so I got an extra ride.

That evening, when Mommy and Daddy returned, they brought us all hamburgers from the A&W. As we ate dinner, Mommy described the beautiful redwood furniture she and Daddy had picked out for our deck. "The store is going to deliver it tomorrow," said Daddy.

Deck 'n Dock was really beginning to feel like home.

7 "HELP, WE'RE GONNA DROWN!"

Well, it was finally here: Summer 1967, our first whole summer on Hemingway Road. Dad was down state working as the manager of the Ypsilanti Press. He joined us on weekends and on his vacations. Mom and Aunt Maxine had arranged for all of us (except for Stephen as he was too young) to take swimming lessons at Depot Beach in Charlevoix.

Mom awakened Billy and me at 6:30 a.m. in order for us to drive into Charlevoix to pick up Shelley, Scott, and Sheila, and make it to Depot Beach by 8:00 a.m. for swimming lessons.

A man with sunglasses and a whistle summoned everyone into a group. He called out everyone's names and announced that we would be put into groups according to how well we could swim. We all watched while the first person was tested. The man called out several strokes to perform. This went on for ten minutes.

He called out "Billy Hein." My tall, skinny nine-year-old brother waded into the water with all the confidence in the world. He swam all the strokes pretty well. When he was finished, the man said, "You're in the intermediate group."

Sheila and I were both about three and a half feet tall and five years old. As Scott, who was six, was called, Sheila and I held hands and began to worry. We were very good in waist deep water and running through sprinklers, but had never submerged our entire bodies at one time. Scott completed his test and was also put into the intermediate group, as well as Shelley.

I felt safe for the time being because I figured they would call all of the Shepard kids at the same time. Just then, I heard the man say, "Alicia Hein?" Sheila looked relieved, but my heart was pounding! I walked toward the water and waded in. Let me tell you, Lake Charlevoix is no bath at 8:30 a.m.! The man told me what to do and I just stood there looking for my mother, who had apparently gone grocery shopping. After about three minutes of me standing there like a fool, my brother, Billy, who looked sorry for me, said, "She can't swim at all!" The man looked at me, told me to get out of the water, and said, "You will be in the beginners' class." Sheila and I ended up in the beginners' class together.

My mother drove us in and faithfully picked us up every morning. I began to hate swimming! Every morning, the teacher tortured us a little bit more! I was bound and determined not to get my entire head under the water at one time! Did this teacher think we were fish?

It was mid-summer and time to move on into a higher class of swimming instruction. Parents were due to watch tests at 9:00 a.m. The teacher was in no mood to watch us stand in knee deep water and complain today. She finally had us do it--we were told to take a deep breath and float on our stomachs. I think she called it "Dead Man's Float." Was she serious? She wanted us to do something that a dead man would do?

Well, I tried it while she held her hands underneath my stomach. I immediately got water up my nose, sprang up and began to cry. Other children seemed to be doing okay. Then it was Sheila's turn. The teacher offered to put her hands under her stomach to hold her up, too. Much to the teacher's dismay, I blurted out, "It doesn't help! I almost drowned!"

Sheila decided not to try this Dead Man's Float at all!

It was time for our swimming tests to start and parents were arriving. The wind was really starting to pick up and the water was getting rough! White caps were starting to form on the lake. The older kids had their tests first. They all swam out to the diving platform and performed everything they had learned over the past four weeks. Shelley, Scott, and Billy passed with flying colors into advanced intermediate.

By the time it was our turn to take the test, in my mind, the lake was almost violent. The sand had churned up in the water, making it look like gloom and doom. The sun had disappeared behind the clouds.

The instructor moved a picnic table from the beach out into the water so we could dive from a bench, already submerged. About two kids out of ten succeeded with this task. The water had just gotten too rough!

Sheila and I ended up holding hands standing on the picnic bench with waves crashing on us whining together. The tests were over and we had failed: We were still "beginners."

Our parents were so proud of Shelley, Scott, and Billy! Uncle Jim and my Dad imitated Sheila and me as a joke, as if we were not humiliated enough already! Dad later comforted me by telling me that he was not a champion swimmer, either, and that, in time, I too would learn to swim.

8 THE COUSINS ARE LOST AT SEA

Mackinac Island is a beautiful little island in Northern Michigan. It is covered with quaint little summer cottages and is only lived on in the summer months. There are several resort hotels, but the most famous hotel on the island is The Grand Hotel. Several movies have been filmed at The Grand Hotel. The hotel is just what it says it is: GRAND! Its six hundred sixty foot long veranda is the largest porch or veranda in the United States. The Grand Hotel is white with many pillars across the veranda. It sits high up on a hill with dignity. The swimming pool is also very large. When you are a guest there, you are treated like royalty. You are assigned the same waiter in the dining room throughout your stay.

Another unique thing about Mackinac Island is that there are no motorized vehicles allowed. They use horses, buggies, and bicycles for transportation. To get onto the island, you must take a ferry over from Mackinaw City, which is about a twenty-minute ride. You may also take your own boat over to the island. It is very peaceful to hear the horses "clompety-clomp" instead of noisy cars. My personal favorite shop on the island is Murdick's Fudge. You can watch them make it on large marble slabs.

My Aunt Maxine, Uncle Jim, and my parents planned a trip for us to Mackinaw Island. My Uncle Jim owned a cabin cruiser named The Blue

Max. He also had some friends who owned cabin cruisers who were going to go to Mackinac Island with us. His friend, Andy, had a cabin cruiser named Tim Tom. His other friend, Art, and his family had a boat named Pinar. They were all going by boat from Round Lake in Charlevoix to Mackinac Island. My parents told my aunt and uncle that our family would drive to Mackinaw City and take a ferry over to the island and that we would meet them there. Billy and I wanted to go on The Blue Max with our cousins and Grammy.

"You just be happy that you can sleep over on the Blue Max when we get there," said Dad.

We all met over on the island. We rented bikes, swam in The Grand Hotel's swimming pool and took a horse and buggy ride. We had a terrific weekend. It went by so quickly! We were all sad when it was time to leave.

"Karel?" asked Uncle Jim. "Why don't you let Billy and Alicia ride back to Charlevoix in the boat with us?"

My dad looked over at my mom and shook his head, "no."

"Jim, you have enough to handle with your four kids. Billy and Alicia may go back the way they came," said Dad.

Billy and I were disappointed! Mom asked Grammy to ride home with us if she wasn't up to the bouncy boat ride back to Charlevoix. Grammy said that she would go back on The Blue Max because all her things were on it and it would be easier to leave things the way they were.

Dad bought our ferry tickets back to Mackinaw City. We hugged everyone goodbye and boarded the ferry. We left the dock and I overheard my dad talking to my mom.

"It looks like rain."

"What a miserable trip back to Charlevoix they're going to have if it rains," Mom replied.

As we got out of the harbor into the wide part of the lake, the large ferry really bounced around! The water had become very rough.

"Jim said that he had checked with the Coast Guard for conditions back to Charlevoix and they had said it would be fine," assured my dad.

"Well, I'm glad we didn't let Billy and Alicia go home with them. I still think it's awfully rough," said Mom.

We made it back to Mackinaw City, loaded the car and headed back to Deck 'n Dock. We arrived home at 12:00 p.m. Noon. Around 2:00 p.m., Mom called Uncle Jim's marina in Charlevoix to see if The Blue Max and the others had made it home yet. The man at the marina said that they hadn't and he was worried because there were strong gale warnings out.

"They should never have allowed them to leave Mackinac Island under these conditions!"

My mom thanked the man and said that she would keep in touch. Two more hours went by and The Blue Max and the others were nowhere in sight. My dad called the Coast Guard and they said that they had heard from the Blue Max about an hour ago and had lost radio contact with them. They also said that they had already started a search party for them as well as many others and would keep him posted.

Another hour passed and I could tell my parents were very worried!

"Karel, don't worry. I'm sure Jim can handle the rough water!"

My mom started to cry. "The children must be scared to death! And, my mother--I wish she had come with us. Oh, Dear God, what if they go down?"

"There there, Karel," said Dad. "I'm sure the good Lord will see them through this."

I started to cry. The thought of never seeing my cousins, grandmother, aunt and uncle saddened me to the point of nausea!

My dad called the Coast Guard again. "Have you spotted or heard from the Blue Max yet?"

"No, Mr. Hein. It's getting late and it will be dark in a couple of hours. We're doing everything we can."

My dad suggested that we go into Charlevoix to the marina and wait there. My mom didn't want to go; she wanted to stay near our phone. So, Billy and I went with Dad. We waited around the marina for half an hour. Every time the bridge opened, going out into the Lake Michigan, we prayed that it was The Blue Max coming in, but it never was.

"Dad," I said. "Do you think that they have sunk?"

"I hope and pray not, Alicia!" said Dad.

Just then, the bridge opened. A cabin cruiser came bouncing through into Round Lake harbor.

"It's Uncle Jim's friend, Art," said Billy.

"Yes," said Dad. "It's the Ribals."

As they approached the dock at the marina, Mrs. Ribal looked very sick and was ready with the rope. She jumped onto the dock and began to tie up the boat.

"Are you alright?" asked my dad.

"It's a miracle we found our way back!" said a very worn out Mr. Ribal.

"Did you see anything of the others back there?" asked my dad.

"You mean they haven't made it back, yet?" asked Mr. Ribal.

"No," answered my dad.

"It's like a hurricane on the high seas out there! I hope they make it back before dark or they will really be lost!" said Mr. Ribal.

Just then, Mrs. Ribal carried their little girl, Stephanie up from the cabin.

"Is Stephanie okay?" I asked.

"She has been sea-sick for hours and we need to get her home and into bed," said Mrs. Ribal.

My dad called the Coast Guard back and they were still trying to locate several missing boats. Then Dad called Mom and she was frantic by now!

"Come on, kids. We better go home and sit with Mom. If the news is bad, we should all be together."

I felt sick and scared! All we could do then was pray and wait. When we got home, Dad made us some dinner. None of us could eat; we were all too upset! All I could think of were my cousins, scared, lost, maybe even drowning.

Before we got up from the table, the phone rang. It was the Coast Guard.

"Mr. Hein, I'm happy to report to you that the Blue Max and Tim Tom have safely made it to Beaver Island. You will be hearing from them soon."

My dad broke out into a great big smile!

"Thank you, very much!" Dad hung up the phone and blurted out to us, "They're all safe at Beaver Island."

"Oh, thank God!" exclaimed Mom.

We were all so happy that they were safe and sound! The phone rang again and my mom grabbed it in a hurry!

"Hello!"

"Jim, we were so worried," said Mom.

"It was a trip we'll always remember!" said Uncle Jim. "The kids were really tossed around and became very sea-sick."

"Are the rest of you okay?" asked Mom.

"We're alright, but a little shaken from the rough trip. The weather report I got this morning wasn't too accurate," said Uncle Jim. "Did the Ribals make it back?"

"Yes, they did," said Mom. "Give our love to everyone!"

"I'll do that," said Jim.

"When do you think you'll be coming back?" asked Mom.

"Hopefully tomorrow, weather permitting! We'll let you know," said Jim.

"Goodbye," said Mom.

"Goodbye," said Jim.

Mom told us that everything was fine and that they would be home soon.

Thank you, Lord, for saving my Grammy, Uncle, Aunt, and Cousins!

9 THE KENNEDYS ARE COMING!

I love my summers on Hemingway Road, but there aren't a whole lot of children to play with. David Kennedy, who was a year older than me, came up to their cottage about one month each summer. Their cottage was next to *Little Brown House*. Billy, David, and I were compatible, so I always looked forward to the Kennedy's arrival! This meant someone to fish, swim, and goof off with.

"Lishie, go down and get the mail, please," asked Mommy.

"Okay, Mom," I answered.

As I hopped, skipped, and jumped down toward the mailboxes, I heard, "Hi Lishie!"

"Oh, hi Grammy. I didn't see you up there on your porch. I'm going to get our mail; do you want to come with me, Grammy?"

"No, not today, dear. I'll see you when you get back," replied Grammy."

"Okay," I said, skipping away.

I knew every rut, stone, and blade of grass on the road. As I merrily skipped by the Kennedys, I noticed windows open and Mrs. Coblentz's car in the driveway. I stopped dead in my tracks. I knew what that meant--David would be there soon!

I walked up to the cottage and knocked on the screen door. Mrs. Coblentz came to the door.

"Yes, dear. What can I do for you?"

"Are the Kennedys coming soon?"

"Yes, they'll be here on Thursday," replied Mrs. Coblentz.

"Thank you!" I said, as I ran happily all the way to the mailboxes. Thursday was only two days away.

As I walked home, I looked at the Kennedy's cottage. With its windows open, the whole cottage came alive from its long winter of being boarded up and empty. I was elated that my good friend David was on his way to Hemingway Road.

I ran up Grammy's stone steps to *Little Brown House*. "Grammy, guess what?" I asked.

"What?" replied Grammy.

"The Kennedys are coming."

"Oh, that's nice," said Grammy as I handed her mail to her.

"Now David and I can go fishing, biking, swimming, and all the things we have fun doing!"

I ran up the stairs to Deck 'n Dock.

"Shut the screen door Alicia Louise!" Mommy yelled.

"Okay," I answered. "Guess what!"

"What?" asked Mommy.

"The Kennedys are coming on Thursday."

"Good," said Mommy. "It will be nice to see Louise again. Now go out and play and let me get my housework done!"

"Alright," I said.

I was not really a patient person. I did not like the idea of having two whole days to wait until David arrived. Facing the Kennedy's cottage, I sat on the side of our dock and stuck my feet into the water. There was no dock off their beach, no boat, and no beach chairs. But, within a few days, that would all change.

David had two older brothers, Todd and Albie. He also had an older sister named Louie, which was short for Louise.

As I went to bed that night, I thought maybe they would get here a day early. They were driving from Dixon, Illinois, about a nine-hour trip for them. Wednesday was about the longest day I ever experienced! Thursday morning finally came.

"What are you in such a hurry for?" asked Mommy.

"David is coming today. I have to get over there to meet him!" I exclaimed.

"You're going over there to just sit and wait for them?" asked Billy. "That could be hours!"

"Uh-huh!" I yelled. "They'll be here soon!"

"You better pack a lunch!" Billy laughed.

"Stop teasing your sister," demanded Mommy.

I decided to go the back way to the Kennedy's on the wooden path behind *Little Brown House*. I stopped to pick a chive along the way. Grammy had planted those years ago. Where *Little Brown House* ended, so did the brown wooden path. It then turned to a narrow path of cement that led to the Kennedy-Miller cottage. About an hour went by and I had had enough! I went home and Billy asked if I wanted to go swimming. I agreed. Billy got out the giant truck inner tube. We each sat on a side and bobbed up and down. It was especially fun when a big boat went by and made large waves. Mommy was working on her rock garden. A few minutes later, Mommy was talking to someone holding a pan.

"It's Albie!" yelled Billy. We both ran up to greet him.

"Where's David?"

"Hey Billy. Hey Alicia," said Albie. "David has to unpack and then he'll be right over."

"Oh, good!" I said.

"I came over to borrow some ice. That's what the pan is for," said Albie.

"Oh, I'll get it right now!" said Mommy.

Mommy got the ice and Albie said he'd see us later.

"Now Alicia, you stay here until they are finished unpacking!" Mommy said sternly.

"Why? I can help them."

"You just stay here where I can see you!" replied Mommy.

"Oh, alright!" I grumbled.

About a half an hour later, there was a knock on the door. I jumped up. It was David.

"Hi!" I yelled.

"Hi!" He yelled back.

Billy got up to say "Hi!"

"Come on in and have an ice cream cone, David," said Mommy.

"Thanks!" said David.

We talked for a while, and then Billy and I walked David home. "See you tomorrow!" We both said. "Yeah, see ya!" said David. I had to get a good night's sleep because tomorrow would be a very fun, but busy day.

10 THE TROUBLE WITH TAPIOCA

Fourth of July, 1967, the cousins came over to Hemingway Road for the weekend. Mom invited everyone over for dinner on the deck. The adults sat at one end of the deck on the redwood furniture and the kids sat around the umbrella table at the other end. We had Dad's great Webber kettle, barbequed chicken, Mrs. Hammond's corn on the cob, and mashed potatoes. It was always so much fun to be with Aunt Maxine, Uncle Jim and the cousins! We were truly lucky kids to be together on Hemingway Road on the Fourth of July.

"Do you kids want anything else?" asked Mom.

"No thanks!" we shouted in unison.

Billy was telling jokes and being quite a comedian as usual.

"Well, are you kids ready for dessert?"

"YES!" we all said.

Mom and Aunt Maxine cleared away our dishes.

Mom came through one of the screen doors carrying a big tray of desserts. Each pudding dish had a little Fourth of July flag standing in the middle of it. We all started in on our dessert. Much to our dismay, most of us dropped our spoons into our bowls. All of us except, of course, Billy. Billy was tall and skinny, but he would eat anything that was put in front of him!

In fact, he had been known to eat school hot lunches for me. We were taught at St. Paul's that it is a sin to waste food; however, I thought it was sinful to serve bad-tasting food.

"Mommy! What is this stuff? It's yucky!" All the kids started to laugh.

"Alicia Louise!"

Uh-oh. I was in immediate danger of being in serious trouble!

"I worked hard to make you a lovely Fourth of July dessert. It's tapioca pudding."

"But Mommy, it tastes like the paste you used to hang wallpaper!"

All the kids laughed again. Then Aunt Maxine came over to our table and said, "My kids better start enjoying the nice dessert Aunt Karel made now!"

Boy, spoons started clattering.

"You better watch what you say Alicia Louise!" said Mommy.

"Now start eating."

Our parents resumed their conversation.

"Thanks a lot, Lish!" said Shelley.

"Yeah," agreed Scott. Then Sheila and Stephen chipped in their two cents worth.

"Well," I said. "I'm not eating that gunk!"

"You have to!" said Billy.

"Oh, yeah?" I turned to my side and emptied my pudding dish onto the ground below the deck.

"Hey, that's not fair!" said Sheila.

"Lish, throw mine over, too!" Exclaimed Shelley.

Just before Shelley handed her dish to me, Aunt Maxine walked back over to our table.

"Keep up the good work, kids!"

Then she pulled a chair up to our table to talk with us. Now there was no hope to throw anyone else's pudding over the deck.

"Well, Lishie, I see you've eaten all of your pudding," said Aunt Maxine.

"Oh, yes, I guess I liked it after all."

"The rest of you finish up and thank Aunt Karel. Then after awhile, you may all go swimming tonight and do sparklers.

"Yay!" We all exclaimed. It was a treat to go swimming at night! Aunt Maxine got up and went inside.

"Lish we ought to make you eat some of this goo!" Said Scott.

"You always get away with everything!" Said Billy.

"Well, I can't help it if I'm so smart! Why don't you eat their pudding since you like it so much?" I asked.

"Because we're being watched now, Einstein," said Billy.

Everyone finished except little Stephen. Aunt Maxine came back out.

"Everyone can go swimming except Stephen. He hasn't finished yet."

Then Stephen had a big tantrum and Aunt Maxine took him next door to *Little Brown House* to put him to bed.

"Let's get our suits on and go swimming!" Said Billy.

"Okay, we'll meet at the beach," said Scott.

When Aunt Maxine came back, I heard Mommy tell her that she felt badly about little Stephen being punished.

"You know I don't put up with that kind of stuff," said Aunt Maxine. "He'll be just fine."

"Still the same," said Mommy. "I promise I'll never make tapioca pudding again!"

"It's okay, Karel. We loved it," said Aunt Maxine.

As we met on the beach, I noticed a cold shoulder from everyone.

"What's the matter?" I asked.

"Poor Stephen is up in his room looking out the window at us because he didn't eat his pudding," said Shelley.

"I know. I feel bad," I said.

"Well, you shouldn't be allowed to swim, either," said Billy. "You didn't finish your pudding."

"Sheila, are you mad at me?"

"Yes, I am."

"Well, then I will punish myself and not go swimming either."

"Don't you tell Mom!" Shouted Billy.

I couldn't go back up to Deck 'n Dock or the adults would ask me why I wasn't swimming. So, I thought, I would sneak into *Little Brown House* and visit Stephen.

"Hi Stephen!"

"Oh, hi Lishie," said Stephen in a happy tone.

"I'm sorry I got you in trouble."

"I know," said Stephen who sat on his cot. Just then I heard someone come upstairs. I was scared because I wasn't supposed to interrupt Stephen's punishment.

"Hi Stevie, it's Grammy."

"Oh, thank goodness it's you, Grammy!"

"Is that you Lishie?" Grammy asked—it was dark.

"Yes, Grammy!"

I told her what happened and she gave us both a hug.

"Well, I won't tell anyone," said Grammy. "I think you've both been punished enough!"

"Yeah," said Stephen. "And, I'm the only one who has an 'uncomprable' bed."

Grammy and I both laughed and hugged Stephen.

"Everyone's mad at me, Grammy."

"They'll forget all about it tomorrow," said Grammy.

"I love you, Grammy!"

"I love you, too," said Grammy.

11 DAVID RENTS A ROW BOAT

As we were having breakfast, Mrs. Kennedy was walking up to our door.

"Hello Louise!" Said Mom.

"Hello Karel!" Said Mrs. Kennedy.

"So, how have all the Heins weathered the winter?"

"Just fine," answered Mom. "How about the Kennedy's winter?" asked Mom.

"We survived the cold very nicely," said Mrs. Kennedy.

"Hello Alicia. You have grown at least an inch since last summer."

"Hi Mrs. Kennedy. Is David up yet?"

"Oh, yes. He is having his breakfast. The reason I came over is to ask you, Karel, if Alicia can go across the lake with us to Scott's. I'm going to rent a row boat for David and wondered if Alicia could ride in the row boat back with David across the lake."

"That would be fine as long as she wears her life jacket," said Mom.

"Oh, good!" I said.

I went back to the Kennedys with David's mother and we drove to the

Ironton Ferry. We walked aboard and sat on the black bench. A couple of cars drove onto the ferry. The "gate puller" closed the big iron gates and we started across the lake. I loved watching the big ferry cables disappear under the water as we crossed the lake. Turk, the ferry operator, collected thirty-five cents from each car. We did not have to pay since we were pedestrians. As we docked, the big iron gates were pulled down and the cars drove off. We walked off and went into Scott's. They sold all kinds of fishing gear, bait, rented boats, and my favorite, the many jars of penny candies. I sat on one of the red metal stools and selected two pieces of bazooka bubble gum, two caramel-nut squirrels, and two tootsie rolls. Six cents was my total purchase. I handed Mrs. Scott six pennies and she handed me a tiny brown paper bag with my candy inside.

Mrs. Kennedy rented one of their yellow row boats. She walked us out onto the dock and made sure I had put my life jacket on. David had a life jacket next to him. He was a terrific swimmer and wearing the life jacket would have made it hard for him to row the boat.

"Now David, stick to the shoreline instead of coming across the middle of the lake."

"Okay mother, I will," replied David.

As we pushed off the dock, David started rowing.

Our cottages looked far away along Hemingway Road. The lake was always calm by the ferry as was the South Arm of the lake because it is not a wide body of water. It got a little rougher as we rowed farther away from the ferry.

"I better head for the shoreline before my mother has the binoculars on us," said David.

I was enjoying my candy.

"Here, David, have a tootsie roll."

"Okay, but you have to try a piece of my hot tamale candy."

"I've never had those. I don't like hot-tasting stuff," I said.

"They're not that hot," said David. "See? They're great!" David popped several into his mouth.

"Okay, I'll try one."

It wasn't bad at first, but then the fire on my tongue ignited.

"Ouch! This is way too hot," I exclaimed as I spit the candy out into the lake. I then scooped up some lake water into my mouth.

David was laughing so hard, he had to stop rowing for a moment.

"Real funny!" I yelled.

"No, you're funny!" laughed David.

"I can't believe I drank lake water!"

I swooped some water from the lake onto David.

"Oh, yeah? Now you're going to get it!" said David. He then splashed me with an oar. I was drenched.

"Okay, okay, I surrender!"

"That's good, because you'll never win at this game!"

"The lake is getting a little choppy. I'll get closer to the shoreline."

"Hey, what are these neat things for?" I asked.

"They're built-in fish holders so that we don't need a stringer when we catch fish," said David. "Lift the top up."

"Neat. There's water in there from the lake so the fish can swim."

"Yup," said David.

We were already in front of the Porter cottage. They were lucky because they had all sand on their beach and no rocks like we had.

"Hey, it looks like Albie is putting our dock out," said David.

"Then you can put your motor boat out," I said.

"I'm going to learn how to water ski this year," said David.

"Really? I can't even swim very well yet," I replied.

"Well, I'm a great swimmer. You can be our observer when I go skiing."

"Okay, I will."

We went by the Webbs', Harkness', Hargraves' and Bulls' and were finally approaching the Kennedys' cottage.

"That's a pretty spiffy rowboat you have there, Dave," said Albie.

"Yup, it's spiffy alright," David agreed.

"Hey Dave, I can use your help this afternoon," said Albie.

"Okay," said David.

"I'll see you later on. I have to tell my mom that we are back."

"Okay," said David.

"Do you want to go fishing later?"

"Sure!"

"Come and get me when you are finished at the dock."

"Okay, see you later."

I went home and got my fishing pole, bait box and the net ready at our beach. Mom was raking the sand on the beach and Grammy was putting beach chairs in a circle.

"What are you guys doing?" I asked.

"We are having a little cook-out on the beach for the Kennedys tonight," said Mom.

"Oh, that sounds like fun."

"Well, I know that they just arrived and there's so much to do with opening a cottage, so that's why I invited them over."

"That's nice of you, Mom," I said. "David and I are going fishing in a little while."

"Well, catch some big ones!" Mom said.

Just then, I saw David rowing over toward our dock.

"Are you ready to catch some fish?" asked David.

"I am always ready to catch some fish," I said.

The lake was calm and we could see the bottom of the lake very clearly.

"Which rock pile?" asked David.

"Let's try the second one," I suggested.

"The second one it is."

We rowed over rock-pile number one.

"Tell me when to stop."

"STOP!" And with that, David threw out an anchor and we were exactly over the second rock pile. We reached for our poles and I opened the bait box.

"Here you go, David."

"Wow! There are a ton of night crawlers in there."

"My dad left a bunch last weekend but he said to split them in half since they are so big."

"Okie-dokie," said David. He split one and handed me the other half.

"Yuck!" I yelled.

"I thought you got over worms being yucky last summer."

"I did, but splitting them in half is so gross!"

"I'm already getting some nibbles," said David.

"Me too," I said.

"I got one!" yelled David.

I looked at his pole and it was really bent over.

"Reel it in!" I yelled.

"I am!" David yelled back. He brought it into the boat.

"It's a pretty nice-sized perch," I said.

"I'd say about twelve inches," said David.

It was flip-flopping all over the bottom of the boat. David took the fish off the hook and put it into the fish holder.

"Yikes, I'm getting bitten by mosquitoes," I said.

"I know; so am I. We should have used some bug repellant. Our mothers are gathering on the beach. There could be trouble," said David.

"No, there's not. We're having a cook-out together."

"I know. I'm just joking around."

Just then, I got a huge bite. I reeled in the biggest rock bass I'd ever seen. They're usually pretty small.

"That's a nice-sized 'rocky'," said David.

"David, I still hate taking the fish off the hook."

"Okay. Bring that thing-a-ma-jig over here." David used a lot of funny words. "You hooked him through the gill."

"Well, take the hook out of the gill."

"I'm attempting just that, but I don't want to kill it. I got it out, but it doesn't look too good."

"Put him in the holding place."

"Okay, he's in."

"Kids, c'mon in for dinner in a few minutes!" yelled Mom.

"Okay Mom!" I yelled back.

David opened the fish-holding compartment.

"Your fish is floating on top of the water," said David.

"Oh, darn. That's the biggest rock bass I'd ever caught."

"Well, now it's the deadest rock bass you'd ever caught."

After pronouncing the fish dead, David flung my large rock bass out into the lake.

"David!" yelled his mom. "It's time to come in for dinner!"

"Yes, Mother! We're coming in!" yelled David.

David pulled up the anchor and rowed over to his beach.

"I think I'll let the fish I caught go since he's the only one we caught that's still alive."

"That's very funny!" I said.

David threw his fish back into the lake. We walked over to our beach. Hamburgers and hot dogs were always good cooked on an open fire. After we finished dinner and ended the evening with friends and family, I knew there was a lot more fun like this to come this summer on our Hemingway Road!

12 THE WITCH OF HEMINGWAY ROAD

David, Billy and I were off to our usual summer antics and activities. There were eleven cottages along Hemingway Road. One of them was a log house, buried behind trees and hidden away. It had a big crystal ball in the front yard. It was eerie and downright spooky! I heard my parents say that there was no inside plumbing, just an outhouse. The rest of the old cottages had had indoor plumbing for years.

The little old lady who lived there was named Edith Harris. What a creepy name. She was about four feet, three inches tall and bent over a cane. You could spot her walking down the road, usually to borrow someone's telephone because she had no electricity or modern appliances. It wasn't because she was poor. She was left over from the pioneer days and did not adapt to modern conveniences.

I saw her once at Grammy's using the telephone. I popped in to say hi to Grammy and stopped suddenly in my tracks when I heard a low scratchy voice. I was shocked. Why was the phone down inside the front of her dress? I ran up to Grammy and kind of hid behind her.

"Grammy?" I asked.

"Yes dear?" she replied.

"Why did Edith have the phone down her dress?"

"Well, you see," said Grammy. "Edith is hard of hearing so she has a hearing aid that she wears around her neck to help her hear."

"Oh, that's really kind of scary," I replied.

"Why do you say that?" asked Grammy.

"She just does everything so strangely."

"Just because someone does something a little differently doesn't make them scary," answered Grammy. "There's a lot that Miss Harris has accomplished in her life. Maybe you should get to know her better."

"No thanks. She reminds me of a witch!"

"Alicia Louise!" exclaimed Grammy. "That's not nice at all!"

"I know, Grammy, but that's how I feel."

"Well, I think you better feel differently about this."

"I'll try, Grammy," I said. "I'm going over to David's now."

"Okay dear. I'll see you later."

"Bye Grammy."

I found David wading into the lake on their beach.

"Hi David."

"Hi!" He shouted back.

"Do you want to go for a bike ride?" I asked.

"Sure." He replied.

David always rode me on the handlebars of my brother's red Stingray bicycle. We traveled many miles this way during the summer. He was a really good driver and I trusted him completely.

As we rode down Hemingway Road, I told him about how I saw Edith today at Grammy's and how she had spooked me. A couple of minutes later, we were in front of Edith's cottage. All of a sudden, David turned into her driveway and we spilled over. David ran away.

I looked up and saw Edith staring at me from her porch. Then I saw the large scary crystal ball. I screamed and then ran away, calling for David.

"Why did you do that?" I screamed at the top of my lungs.

"You were so spooked that I thought I'd really spook you."

"Well, you can just laugh your way back to the witch's house to get my brother's bike."

"Okay, okay," laughed David.

As we approached Edith's cottage, the bike was thrown out into the dirt road right before us. We were both shocked! David picked up the bike and we both ran back to his house laughing.

That night when I went to bed, I felt bad because Grammy had told me Edith was a nice person and here she was, a little old lady, who had to pick up a heavy bicycle and throw it into the road. She might have had a heart attack and it would have been David's and my fault. A guilty conscience always haunts.

The next day, Billy and David told me that they had put a garter snake into Edith's mailbox after the mail had come.

"You guys are going to scare that old woman to death!" I yelled. "You're going to be in big trouble."

"No we're not," answered Billy. "You said she was a witch and witches love snakes!"

"They do?" I asked.

Billy and David laughed.

Later, we learned through other neighbors that Edith had found the snake and threatened to call the police.

Luckily, my father and David's father talked to Edith and explained that Billy and David had just played a foolish prank and promised it would not happen again.

The next day, Grammy took Billy, David and me down to Edith's cottage.

"I'm scared, Grammy!" I said.

"Stop that nonsense!" said Grammy. "Edith asked that I bring you children for a visit today and I expect all of you to be well-behaved and polite."

"We will," we said in unison.

When we got to Edith's there were five chairs on her long concrete porch.

"Sit down, please," said Miss Harris. "The reason I have asked you here today is to tell you about myself. I, too, was a youngster on Hemingway Road when I was growing up."

"You were?" I asked.

"Yes, I was. In fact, the road was almost named Harris Road instead of Hemingway Road. Have all of you seen the large railroad bridge over Round Lake in Charlevoix?"

"Yes," we all answered.

"Well, you see, my father designed that bridge."

"Wow!" exclaimed Billy.

"Isn't that amazing?" asked Grammy.

"Yes, it is," said Billy.

"When I was younger, I told stories to children at many different libraries throughout the years," added Miss Harris.

"Could you tell us some of your stories someday?" I asked.

"I would be happy to," replied Miss Harris. "You could come by on a rainy day when you can't go swimming and I'll tell you some good stories."

"Okay, we will," I said. "I'm sorry we weren't very nice to you. You're very nice and you're nothing like a witch at all!"

"Oh, Alicia!" said a mortified Grammy.

Miss Harris chuckled. "That's quite alright, Alice," she said to Grammy.

David and Billy apologized too.

We went home and I was never afraid of Edith Harris again.

13 MY SIXTH BIRTHDAY AT LITTLE BROWN HOUSE

It was nearing the end of July, which meant that my birthday was coming up fast. Mom was folding clothes in her bedroom.

"Mommy?"

"Yes Alicia?"

"What are we going to do for my birthday?"

"Your birthday? Do you have a birthday coming up?" Mommy asked in a funny voice.

"You know my birthday is five days away on July 27th. Besides, I saw the wrapped presents on your closet shelf."

"Why Alicia Louise, stay out of my closet," said Mom abruptly. "I'm sure whatever we do, it'll be fun. Now, don't ask any more questions. Go play!"

"Okay, but David went to watch his mom play golf in Boyne City."

"Well, go find something else to do."

"Oh, alright," I grumbled.

Wednesday morning finally came. It was a beautiful sunny day. I ran upstairs to have breakfast.

"Happy birthday, Lishie!" yelled Mom and Billy.

"Thanks!"

They had a special breakfast set up for me.

"I wish dad could be here."

"Well, he will call you tonight, honey. Now, hurry and get ready for swimming lessons," said Mom.

"You mean I have to take swimming lessons on my birthday?" I asked.

"Why sure. Then Grammy, Billy and I will celebrate your birthday tonight."

I went to get ready, but I wasn't real excited. I was really hoping for a birthday party with other kids, not just Mom, Gram and Billy.

As we drove through Charlevoix to pick up the cousins for swimming lessons, we noticed the bridge opening.

"Oh, darn," said Mom. "Now we'll be late."

"It's the 'Beaver Islander'," said Billy.

It swiftly passed under the bridge, out the channel by the "Weathervane Hotel" on its way to Lake Michigan and Beaver Island. It was a big white ferry with green clovers painted on each side of the bow. The bridge slowly lowered and we went to the top of Bridge Street towards the cousins' house.

As my cousins piled into the car, Aunt Maxine waved at the door. The car was quiet.

"Hey, did you guys know today is my birthday?" I asked.

"It is?" asked Shelley. "Well, happy birthday!"

The rest of the kids giggled.

"What's so funny?" I asked.

"Oh, nothing," said Shelley. "You know how they'll laugh over anything!"

She nudged Scott in the ribs.

"Ouch!" yelled Scott.

"Now, you kids be good, okay?" asked Mom. "We're almost there."

When we arrived at Depot Beach, I saw Shelley whisper to Sheila.

"Hey, that's not polite!" I said.

They both laughed and I stormed off in the direction of my class. All through swimming class, Sheila tried to be nice to me, but I was mad because she and Shelley were telling secrets. After swimming, Mom picked us up. The car was quiet. I then heard more giggling and noticed that Mom went right by the cousins' house without dropping them off.

"Mom, you passed their house!" I blurted.

"Happy Birthday, Lish!" They all shouted.

"What's going on?" I asked.

"We're all going back to the cottage for your all-afternoon birthday party," said Mom.

"Oh, wow!" I said. "You guys all fooled me!"

"Boy, you were really mad at me," said Sheila.

"I'm sorry," I said.

"That's okay," she replied. "I was fooling you!"

"David is coming to your party, too," said Mom.

"I think Lish loves David!" Billy laughed.

"Shut up, Billy, I do not!"

"Billy, don't tease your sister today. It's her birthday."

"Okay, I won't," he agreed.

When we got to the Ironton Ferry, we lucked out because it was on our side. Mom drove onto the ferry and then started digging through her purse for her ferry coupons.

"Can we get out?" asked Billy.

"No you may not," answered Mom. "We'll be across the lake in a few minutes."

We arrived back at the cottages and got out of the car.

"The party is over at Grammy's."

"How come?" I asked.

"So we could hide it from you!" Mom replied.

We all ran over to *Little Brown House* and Grammy greeted us at the porch door.

"Hi kids. Happy birthday Lishie," said Grammy.

"Thank you!" I shouted.

The big picnic table on the porch was decorated with streamers and balloons. There were party favors, and a birthday cake in the shape of a circus elephant in the middle of the table. It was beautiful. Mom made a turtle-shaped cake for Billy's birthday. His birthday was on July 1st.

We had a great lunch—hamburgers, potato chips, cake and ice cream!

After lunch, it was time to open presents. I got great gifts! Everyone, including me, got a kick board for the lake, the boys each got a toy car and the girls got paper dolls.

After we were done opening presents, we put our bathing suits on and went down to the beach with our new kick boards, inner tubes and baskets of beach toys. Grammy and Mom sat on the beach and watched us. What a great party!

Uncle Jim and Aunt Maxine came over to pick up the cousins.

I was ready for bed that night, when Daddy called from Ypsilanti to wish me a Happy Birthday, and to remind me that he would be there in a few days.

14 VENETIAN FESTIVAL

It was the middle of July 1967. Mom still drove us into Charlevoix faithfully every morning for swimming lessons. For the next few weeks we would be staying in town while Mom and Aunt Maxine worked on the float for the annual Venetian Festival. Shelley, Scott and Billy usually "ditched" Sheila, Stephen and me. We really didn't mind much because there was always something exciting we could find to do at the marina.

Many boats were kept at the marina: Cabin cruisers, speed boats, sail boats, and even some row boats. My favorite place at the marina was the big barn over the water used to house and protect the larger boats. There were several docks under the big barn roof. On the outside, the big barn was yellow with a green roof and a Gulf Gas emblem on the side of it. There were docks, big ropes, and boat bumpers along the sides of the docks.

Round Lake was filled with boat marinas and docks and downtown Charlevoix was right off Round Lake. While Mom and Aunt Maxine were busy making flowers out of red, white and blue tissue paper for the float, Sheila, Stephen and I went out in their little sport yak—a lifeboat. We were rowing around Round Lake looking at all of the boats.

"Hey!" I said. "There's Lady Lou!"

Just then the loud sputtering of Lady Lou's engines started up and startled us! Sheila began rowing very rapidly! When we were far enough away, we burst into laughter! Lady Lou goes by our cottage all the time and when she does, she makes great big, giant waves.

"Those engines sure are loud enough," remarked Sheila.

"Yeah, like a bomb exploding!" I replied.

As I looked around Round Lake, I could see the Beaver Islander; the Coast Guard cutter, "Sundew"; and many cottages, some of which were Mr. Young's "mushroom houses." They were called that because the roofs resembled mushrooms. Also, the little town of Charlevoix was so pretty from the water.

We decided to go back to the marina and check on the progress of the float. We were excited because we would all be riding in the float for the Venetian Parade. As we approached Aunt Maxine and Mom, we noticed that they had made about a thousand tissue flowers.

"Wow!" I exclaimed. "You must almost be finished!"

"No, we're not," answered Mom.

"We have a long ways to go yet," said Aunt Maxine.

"We're bored," said Sheila.

"Well, you two girls can go into the marina and dust off merchandise," said Aunt Maxine.

"Oh, yuck," replied Sheila.

"One…two…three!" said Aunt Maxine in a stern voice.

"Okay, okay, we're going!" said Sheila.

Mom, Billy and I went into Charlevoix every day for the next two weeks to finish the float.

There were four more days until the parade. Billy and Scott went next door to the Crosse's Fishery to watch the men clean the big fish they caught. I did not like to go there because of the strong smell of fish.

As Sheila and I dusted off merchandise in the marina, Uncle Jim walked in.

"Good job, girls."

"Thanks," we said together.

Uncle Jim was busy waiting on customers. By 5:00pm, Mom drove us back to Hemingway Road so she could get busy cleaning and preparing for our friends who would be visiting for a week. The Van Schoicks from Jackson, Michigan would be arriving on Friday night. The Van Schoicks had been good friends of my parents for years. They had three children: Tim, Tad, and Debbie. Dad would also be arriving on Friday night. The parade was on Saturday.

The Venetian Festival consisted of various activities. In the park around Round Lake, there would be a pet and doll show held near the trout pond. Then there was the parade and all kinds of contests. At night, there would be a boat parade in Round Lake harbor.

Friday morning was here, the last day before the parade. Grammy was coming with us today to help with the float. Uncle Jim picked us up from Depot Beach swimming lessons and brought us back to the marina where Grammy had a picnic of peanut butter and banana sandwiches and potato chips for lunch.

"Now, don't you children bother your mothers. They have a lot to finish in a small amount of time," said Grammy.

"Okay, Grammy, we won't," replied Shelley.

Shelley was good at keeping us all in line when she had to.

By 4:00pm, the float was finished. It was beautiful!

We were back at Hemingway Road by 5:00pm. Grammy invited us to *Little Brown House* for dinner. She made fried perch, corn bread and green beans. We ate on her big screened porch. There was such a pretty view of the lake from there.

"Let me help you with the dishes, Mom," said our mom.

"No, Karel, you have company coming. Lishie, can help me if she wants to," said Grammy.

"Of course I'll help you Grammy!" I exclaimed. I helped Grammy dry the last dish and then we sat on the screened porch. The lake was so calm as the beautiful orange and pink tinted sun set over it. There were a few boats out on the lake making their perfect "hum."

"Well, Lishie, are you excited about your guests arriving?"

"I can hardly wait!" I exclaimed. "Oh, look Grammy, you can see the fish jumping for bugs."

"Yes, I see that," said Grammy.

"It makes me want to get my fishing pole," I said.

A couple of minutes later, we heard people walking on the deck over at Deck-n-Dock. Daddy and the Van Schoicks had arrived.

"You run along," said Grammy.

"Okay, bye Grammy," I said.

"Goodbye dear," she replied.

I ran up to our cottage.

"Hi Debbie!"

"Hi Lisha!" She answered back.

Debbie was the youngest of the Van Schoicks. She was so cute. She was two years old. Tad was four and Tim was my age. Their father was a pediatrician. Their mom's name was Judy and best of friends with my mom. They had lived next door to each other in Ann Arbor. The Van Schoicks now lived in Jackson, Michigan about forty-five minutes from Ann Arbor.

Mommy was busy setting everyone up for the night. Tim and Tad were bunking in with Billy. Debbie was sleeping with me and their parents were sleeping upstairs on the hide-a-bed.

When I was awakened Saturday morning, I smelled coffee, bacon and eggs. As I looked over a Debbie, she opened her big brown eyes.

"Hi Lisha!" She said.

"Good morning, Debbie," I replied.

"Let's go upstairs for breakfast," I said. I got out of bed and she followed me. Up the stairs we went.

"Good morning, girls," Mrs. Van Schoick said.

"Good morning!" We answered back.

The boys were already up.

It was a beautiful sunny day for the parade. I was so excited I could hardly stand it! The parade was to start at 1:00pm. We left Hemingway Road at about 11:15am to go to the marina in Charlevoix. When we got there, the float with a boat and a snowmobile was hooked on a trailer behind Uncle Jim's station wagon. My cousins and I were all dressed alike in sailor outfits and hats, ready to ride on the float. My parents and the Van Schoicks left to go watch the parade. Uncle Jim and Aunt Maxine would be driving us in the parade route.

As we arrived at our spot in the parade, Aunt Maxine and Uncle Jim helped us out of the station wagon and into the float. Aunt Maxine told each of us where to stand and handed each of us a box of Rain-Blow bubble gum to throw out to spectators. My box was grape.

"Kids, throw out a little handful of gum as we move by everybody," instructed Aunt Maxine. "Shelley, you kind of watch over everyone, okay?"

"I will, Mom," replied Shelley.

As we started moving, I couldn't believe how many people were on the sidelines. About ten minutes later, Aunt Maxine yelled from the car, "Kids, Aunt Karel, Uncle Bill, Grammy and the Van Schoicks are on the left of the float!" We all rushed to the left side of the boat and it's a good thing we weren't really in the water or we might have capsized!

There stood Tim, Tad and Debbie. We all threw big handfuls of gum to them. I saw Mom, Dad and Grammy and waved to them. Grammy caught my eye and blew me a kiss. She always knew how to make me feel good!

When the parade was over, we went back to the marina. There were all kinds of festivities going on in the park: The doll contest and the greased poll contest. That afternoon, we all sat in The Blue Max to watch the afternoon's activities from Round Lake. Sheila and I watched men climb a greased pole for a fifty dollar bill that was at the top of the pole. We were then instructed to take a nap below so that we would not be tired for the boat parade that night. The bow of The Blue Max was a big bed. As we laid down toward the pointed bow on the white cushions, the gentle waves must have rocked us to sleep. After an hour, the Van Schoicks and my family were ready to go back to Hemingway Road.

"We'll see you tonight, Bill," said Uncle Jim. "In fact, we'll come out to the cottages and pick you up in the boats. That way you won't have to worry about the ferry closing."

"Thanks Jim," said Dad.

"Okay, Bill. We'll be out about 6:30. It'll be a nice ride. I'll have Andy bring his boat, too, for the Van Schoicks."

"Sounds great!" said Dad.

We were only back at Deck-n-Dock for a couple of hours when we were all getting ready for another trip back into Charlevoix, only this time by cabin cruiser. The lake was calm and the sun was setting as we all waited on the beach. Dad said, "I hear the boats." Then, in the glare of the setting sun, both the Tim Tom and the Blue Max came bouncing beautifully in front of Hemingway Road. The Tim Tom was owned by friends of Uncle Jim and Aunt Maxine.

The Van Schoicks boarded the Tim Tom and then Uncle Jim pulled the Blue Max up to our dock. Grammy, Mom, Dad, Billy and I boarded and both of the boats turned back toward Charlevoix and traveled side by side back to Round Lake.

We all waved to each other boat to boat as we made our trip back into town.

By the time we arrived at the entrance to Round Lake at the railroad bridge, it was almost dark. We tied up back at the marina. The boat parade wouldn't start for another hour or so. Both boats were tied together so that we could go back and forth. We enjoyed soda, pretzels and chips while our parents enjoyed cocktails. We were all anticipating the boat parade and fireworks. Round Lake was lit up tonight like no other night during the year.

When the boat parade started, we all sat in awe of the beautiful display of boats and lights. There was an old giant sailboat and all kinds of lights on it. It was kind of crazy-looking and Chinese lanterns hung everywhere on it. "It is called a Chinese Junk," said Uncle Jim.

After the festivities were over, Uncle Jim took all of us home to Hemingway Road in the Blue Max.

This was a very special Venetian Festival! I will always remember it!

15 THE IRONTON FERRY

I have briefly mentioned the Ironton Ferry, but have not totally explained its importance to everyone in Ironton and surrounding cities. There are four cities around Hemingway Road in which we do our shopping and go to church: Petoskey, Boyne City, East Jordan, and of course Charlevoix. To get to Charlevoix quickly, you must take the ferry. To get to Boyne City, East Jordan or Petoskey, you do not have to take the ferry. The Ironton Ferry holds up to four cars at one time, two on each side. It takes about five minutes to cross the small section of the South Arm of Lake Charlevoix. You can see the Ironton Ferry very well from Hemingway Road. It's fun to use the binoculars, especially if you're waiting for a guest to arrive. You can walk from Deck-n-Dock to the ferry in about twenty-five minutes. The ferry has big iron gates that must be pulled down before you can drive onto it. Sometimes the county hires high school or college boys to do this job. The ferry was led by heavy cables across the lake and made the most wonderful "chug-a-chug" sound. On a calm night, I could hear it from my bedroom.

There were two different ferry operators, Turk and Jim. They took turns on different shifts. Grammy said that Turk had been running the ferry for years. Jim had not been running the ferry too long, but was so very kind. He would play his mandolin for us if the ferry was not busy. He also taught us how to start the ferry on a trip across the lake. Turk would never let us do that! He was a lot more stern than Jim.

Mom didn't like us hanging out at the ferry because there was a lot of oil and grease from cars on it and we would get dirty. But, we still went there a lot. It was also a great fishing spot!

Boats are not allowed to go fast when they pass by the ferry because of the ferry's cables. On a cold day, we would sit in the little cabin on the ferry. It is really loud inside the cabin when the ferry makes a trip across the lake. Tourists loved the Ironton Ferry and were always taking pictures of it. It really is a one-of-a-kind ferry. Just like everything else, in the winter, the Ironton Ferry has to shut down until spring.

16 TROUBLE AT DEPOT BEACH

It was another gorgeous day in "Charlevoix the Beautiful!" The cousins, Billy and I had just finished our swimming lessons at Depot Beach. Mommy had said that she was going to Oleson's Grocery Store and might be a few minutes late picking us up. I was glad because there was a great playground here at the beach.

"Lish, let's go over to the swings!" Sheila said.

"Yeah, Let's!" I shouted back. I loved running barefoot in the warm sand.

These particular swings were on very long chains and went really high. The view of the lake was fantastic as we swung higher and higher. The glare of the sun across the lake was pretty! Shelley was sitting on a bench waiting and Billy and Scott were punching the tetherball around.

"Uh-oh," said Scott.

"What's the matter?" Billy asked.

"That kid talking to Shelley is the school bully."

"Go away!" We heard Shelley scream.

"C'mon, let's go help her!" Billy said.

"Sheila, look at Billy and Scott. They're running over to Shelley," I said.

ALICIA HEIN COOK

"Yuck!" Sheila exclaimed. "That's Mike. He's mean!"

Sheila and I waited for our swings to slow down some and then bailed from them. We ran toward Shelley, Billy, Scott and the bully.

"You leave her alone!" Billy yelled.

"And just who are you? Her knight in shining armor?" Mike sneered.

"No, I'm her cousin and I said to leave her alone!"

Just then, Mike clenched up his fist and punched Billy right in the eye. Sheila and I stood there in shock!

Shelley yelled to Mike, "Stop it you big bully!"

The two boys began punching and shoving each other. Scott was just about to help Billy when Mommy's big red paneled country squire station wagon pulled up. She jumped out of the car, took one look at Billy's eye and screamed for the boys to "cease and desist" at once!

"Mike the bully" ran away faster than a speeding bullet.

"You kids all get into the car now!" Mommy yelled. As we started on our way, Mommy said she had to stop back at Oleson's to pick up Grammy.

"Just who is that boy?" Mommy asked.

"He's the meanest boy in school!" Scott exclaimed.

"His name is Mike," Shelley said.

"What are you doing fighting that boy, Billy Hein?" Mommy yelled.

"He was helping me, Aunt Karel," explained Shelley. "Mike was picking on me and Billy was trying to make him stop."

"Oh," Mommy sighed. "That's different, then. I'm proud of you, Billy, for defending your cousin!"

"That was very brave of you, Billy," said Shelley.

"It's about time someone stood up to that creep!" Scott said.

76

"He beats up on everyone!" Sheila chimed in.

"Well, it's going to stop!" Mommy said. "A boy should not be allowed to terrorize a whole town of children!"

As we swung by the Oleson's to pick up Grammy, Mommy explained to Grammy what had happened.

"Well," said Grammy. "I sure am glad Billy stood up to that boy! That was a courageous thing to do!"

"Aw, it was nothing," Billy said.

We pulled up to the police station because Mommy wanted to make a report. Shelley gave Mommy all the information about Mike. Grammy sat in the car and waited with us. About twenty-five minutes later, Mommy came out from the station.

"What happened?" Grammy asked.

We were all very quiet so that we could hear.

"Well, the police officer was very nice and he knew exactly who this boy was. He said that he had been in other trouble. They are going to this boy's house to talk to him and his parents."

"Maybe this will stop Mike from being such a bully!" Scott said.

"I sure hope so!" Shelley said.

"Now, before I drop you kids off, how about an ice cream cone?"

"Yeah!" We all shouted.

"Mommy, maybe you should get an extra ice cream for Billy to put on his black eye!" I joked. Everyone started to laugh with me!

17 THE HEMINGWAY SISTERS

Birchmont, named for the many white barked birch trees, was the very last cottage on Hemingway Road. It belonged to the Hemingway's. George Hemingway built the two-story cottage for himself, his wife, and his two daughters, Margaret and Virginia. George, Mr. Hemingway to us children, owned the Hemingway tree farm up behind Hemingway Road and, even though he was no longer with us, to this day, the closed nursery still grows. It contained many straight rows of pine trees, an apple orchard, etc. The two red barns and log-built office stand among overgrown trees and weeds. In the office, you can find everything the way George Hemingway left it; orders on his desk that were never filled, envelopes of seeds with Hemingway Tree Farm printed on them were in abundance. Over in the two red barns were tractors and farm equipment that had been left to rust through the years. Cloth bags of seeds were moth-eaten and half-full. To one end of the barn sat a Model A car, abandoned by time. Billy and I would sit in it and pretend to drive it. The seats were full of holes. My dad had said that mice had eaten the upholstery. The musty smell inside the car was strong. All these things were left behind by the parents of Margaret and Virginia. As the years passed, both Hemingway sisters married. Margaret married Homer Bundy. Virginia married George Spayde. Margaret and Virginia shared Birchmont during the summer, each taking half of the summer, Virginia and George usually taking June and half of July.

I was six years old when I first met the Spaydes. I got up one morning, had breakfast and was just about to leave the room when Mom asked, "Where are you going in such a hurry?"

"I'm going to visit Virginia, Mom. They just arrived yesterday!" I exclaimed. "I'm sure they would love to have some company by now!"

"Well, just don't stay too long," Mom said.

"Okay," I replied.

I went over to Birchmont by using the front road. I passed the Brownlee's Farmhouse and arrived at Birchmont. There was a big bell right outside the front porch door. I knocked on the double white screen porch doors.

"Well, hello. You're Mrs. Shepard's granddaughter, Alicia, aren't you?" Virginia asked.

"Yes," I answered.

"George, Alicia has come to visit us."

"Good afternoon, young lady," George said.

"Hello," I said.

All three of us sat down on the porch. George lit up a big fat cigar.

"How's the fishing been so far this summer?" George asked.

"It's been good!" I answered.

George liked to take the well-varnished row boat out and fish for hours. He never put out the dock or motorboat that was stored in the nursery garage.

Virginia was a petite, pretty lady, but very practical. I liked her very much, but if someone had asked me to choose who I most liked to spend time with, I would have to say Margaret.

The sisters were as different as night and day. I suppose in the older days, they would have described Margaret as "full of spit and vinegar" and Virginia as "prim and proper."

Birchmont looked totally different depending on who was staying there.

When Virginia and George stayed there, it was plain and smelled of liver and onions. When Margaret and Homer arrived, everything came alive. Fresh air permeated through the house. They had a big cup full of candy sticks: Cherry, peppermint, root beer and wintergreen. Laughter instead of sternness filled the air. Virginia and George were very nice but liked their privacy.

After Virginia and George went home, I noticed Mr. Henning's truck over at Birchmont. I skipped cheerfully down their back gravel driveway and knocked on the back screened door. I heard a voice answer, "Howard Henning here!"

"Mr. Henning," I asked. "Are the Bundys coming soon?" He came to the door.

"Hi young lady," He replied. "As a matter of fact, they're coming tomorrow. I'm here with my wife cleaning up so that everything will be ready for them."

"Oh, good!" I yelled. "Goodbye!"

"Goodbye," Mr. Henning said.

Margaret and her husband, also an older couple, were from Tucson, Arizona. They were rich and full of fun! When they first arrived on Hemingway Road, my mother wouldn't let Billy or me go over right away. "Wait 'til they've had time to settle in!" She would say.

The next afternoon, Billy and I wandered over to Birchmont. As we walked up the three steps to their front porch, we were greeted warmly. "Hello dear children!" Margaret cried out. She hugged us both and invited us inside.

"My, how you both have grown! Homer! Billy and Alicia are here."

Homer was a tall kindly white-haired gentleman. "Hello children! Good to see you again." He shook our hands and told us to have a seat.

"Well, Billy," said Homer. "We'll have to call the marina to get the dock, boat, and shore station out." A shore station was a boat lift and most everyone along Hemingway Road had one. Homer had an electric one. Ours, along with everyone else's, was manual. You had to crank the big wheel to lower and raise the boat. Homer also had a welcome light that spun in green, blue, and red lights. It showed boats where the shoreline was at night. It was pretty, too!

"Billy," said Homer. "You're old enough to be captain of my boat this year. Do you think you can handle it?"

"Yes!" Billy exclaimed.

Margaret brought us each a Coke and a bowl of pretzel sticks just like she always did. This was going to be a great summer with the Bundys! Margaret would tell us stories about her children who were now grown and how she spent her summers on Hemingway Road as a little girl with her cousin, famous author Ernest Hemingway.

18 "WE CAN'T WORM OUR WAY OUT OF THIS ONE!"

One of our favorite things to do on Hemingway Road was to go fishing. It was Dad's most favorite pastime. He would always buy night crawlers during the weekends. By the middle of the week when Dad went back down state to work, the worms ran out.

"Mom?" Billy asked. "Could we have 50 cents for a dozen night crawlers?"

"I don't want you kids going over to the ferry to buy them—go dig some up."

So, we went out with a shovel and, after an hour of digging, all we got were about three little, skinny worms."

"We can't catch anything with these!" I exclaimed.

"Hey, I know where we can get some fat night crawlers," Billy said.

"Where?"

"Mr. Bull has a 'worm bed' up by their cabin. We can ask Mr. Bull if we can have some worms."

The Bulls' cabin was used by guests; their main cottage was down by the lake.

"Nobody is here!" I said.

"I know where he keeps the worms," said Billy. "We can tell him we borrowed some after he gets back."

"Are you sure?" I asked.

"Sure!"

So we filled our bait box with a dozen of Mr. Bull's night crawlers.

As we walked back to our dock to go fishing, I had begun to feel badly that we took Mr. Bull's bait without asking.

After about twenty minutes, we didn't even get a bite. I usually loved to fish, but I put my fishing pole down on the dock and walked away.

"Where are you going?" Billy asked.

"I don't feel like fishing anymore!"

"Suit yourself," he said.

About an hour later, Billy came inside.

"Did you catch anything?" I asked.

"Not a bite!" He replied.

"Lishie?" Mom asked. "Will you run next door and tell Grammy that dinner is ready?"

"Okay Mom," I answered. "I'll be right back with Grammy."

During dinner, I felt ill.

"Can't you eat more than that?" Grammy asked.

"I don't feel well," I said. "May I be excused?"

"Alright," said Mom. "Go take your shower and get ready for bed."

After lying in bed for a while, I couldn't get to sleep. I went next door to Billy's room to see if he was asleep yet and he was, so I went upstairs where Mom and Grammy were watching television.

"Why, Lishie, what are you doing out of bed?" Mom asked.

I ran into her arms crying. "Today, Billy and I took worms out of Mr. Bull's worm bed."

"Did you ask to take the worms?" Mom asked.

"No, we were going to, but they weren't home."

"Well, do you think that was the right thing to do?" Mom asked.

"No," I answered, crying. "We didn't even catch any fish."

"Well, there, you see," said Grammy. "Nothing good or positive can come from doing something wrong or dishonest."

"Are you sorry you took the worms?" Mom asked.

"Very!"

"Well, then, you and your brother can go over to the Bulls tomorrow with a dozen night crawlers that we'll buy across the lake to replace the ones you took and apologize."

"Yes, Mom," I answered. "Boy, is Billy going to be mad at me for telling!"

"You just never mind Billy," said Mom. "I'll deal with him."

"Goodnight," I said.

"Goodnight, Lishie," said Mom and Grammy.

The next morning, I awoke to the noise of a boat's motor going across the lake. I felt good until Billy popped his head into my bedroom.

"Thanks a lot, Lish. No one would have known."

Just then, we could hear mom respond, "Except you two and your consciences." She continued. "Get dressed and I'll give you 50 cents to buy some night crawlers and, by the way, 25 cents will be taken out of each of your allowances."

"Let's take bikes over," suggested Billy. "It'll be faster!"

"Okay," I said. "But, wait for me!"

"I will," he promised.

When we got to the Ironton Ferry, the ferry was on the other side, so we had to wait. You could always see our two table umbrellas from the ferry because they were bright orange and yellow.

We rode the ferry over and went to "Scotts'," a shop where you could buy gasoline for your boat, bait, fishing tackle, milk, bread, and a few groceries. Best of all, he sold penny candy! There were six red metal stools in front of the counter. Behind the counter were jars of tootsie rolls, fire balls, squirrels, Bazooka bubble gum, Smarties, jaw breakers, boxes of candy bars, hot tamales, Good'n Plenty, sweet tarts, and more. Last, but not least, was the freezer full of Popsicles, fudge bars and, my favorite, Sno Cones, which were blue, yellow, and red shaved ice.

Mr. and Mrs. Scott, who owned Scott's, lived across the street. They were a nice older couple who had owned the business for years.

I always read the metal sign outside the door before I entered the shop. It said, "I don't know where Mom is, but Pop's on ice," and it showed a bottle of soda pop in a bucket of ice cubes. I thought that was quite funny.

"What can I get for you today?" asked Mr. Scott.

"A dozen night crawlers," said Billy.

"Coming right up."

We followed Mr. Scott outside where there was a big metal tub filled with minnows. Then he opened a refrigerator and pulled out a tray of dirt. He took down a small empty milk carton, cut in half, from a shelf and began pulling night crawlers out of the tray of dirt and put them into the carton. He counted out exactly twelve.

"That will be 50 cents, please," Mr. Scott said.

Billy paid him and we were on our way.

On the way back down Hemingway Road, we stopped several times to skip stones into the lake. I suppose we dawdled because our next stop was the Bulls' house. I was hoping they weren't home, but their green hammock was out and that was a sure sign they were there.

We stepped up onto their porch and, as Billy knocked on the door, I sort of hid behind him. The door opened and Mrs. Bull had a big smile on her face. She always wore her hair up in a bun.

"Come in, children!"

"Is Mr. Bull here?" Billy asked.

"Yes, he's on the sun porch reading the paper."

"Ira?" Mrs. Bull called out. "Billy and Alicia are here to see you."

I thought Ira was such a funny name!

Mrs. Bull's name was Thelma. They had a linen sign that hung on their wall. It read, "Cows may come and cows may go, but the Bull in this house stays on forever." I chuckled to myself and Billy nudged me.

Mr. Bull walked into the room.

"Hi kids!"

"Hello," we quietly answered.

Billy raised the carton of worms.

"What do you have there?" Asked Mr. Bull.

"Mr. Bull," Billy said. "Yesterday, when you were gone, we sort of took some of your night crawlers out of your worm bed and our mom said we should replace them and to tell you we're sorry!"

"Well, I believe you should always ask someone before you borrow anything, but any time I'm here, feel free to come ask me."

"Thank you, Mr. Bull," replied Billy.

"Children, I have some cookies and lemonade for you on the porch," said

Mrs. Bull.

"Thanks!" We said.

After I ate some cookies, I got into the green hammock as I often did. As I lay in the hammock and stared into the beautiful blue sky, I thought, *all's well that ends well—especially on Hemingway Road!*

19 POSITIVELY POISON IVY

Being that this is our first summer in Deck-N-Dock, we were used to our yard at *Little Brown House*. Much to Mom's and Dad's dismay, our yard by the back road was filled with Poison Ivy. I know Dad had bought some kind of tank and sprayer that would spray out Poison Ivy killer. Mom was busy helping Dad pack for his trip back to Ypsilanti for the week.

"I'll be sure to spray the Poison Ivy next week, Karel!" Dad said in a voice of urgency.

"Oh, that will be soon enough," Mom replied. "We just ran out of time this weekend.

"I'm going to come up on Thursday this week so that I can get some extra chores done."

"That'll be great!" Mom exclaimed.

I was glad, too, because I really missed Dad during the week and I felt sorry for him all alone at our other house!

"Dad?" I asked. "Don't forget to bring up my hula hoop next weekend."

"Oh, I sure won't," he promised.

"Make sure you water the trees well. I hear there is almost a drought in Ypsi," said Mom.

"That's on my list, too!" He replied.

Dad packed up his Mustang, hugged us all and was on his way.

The next morning, Billy and I decided to play catch with the kick ball by the back road between *Deck-N-Dock* and *Little Brown House*. I complained because I only had flip-flops on and Billy always made me chase the ball.

"You get it this time!" I yelled.

"Oh, alright!" He grumbled, swooping down to pick up the ball with both hands.

After about a half an hour of this, we quit the boring game.

"Kids, come on in for lunch," Mom called.

We enjoyed some grilled cheese sandwiches and then Mom gave us a list of chores to do.

"By the way, kids, stay out of the Poison Ivy out back until your father sprays it!"

"Okay," we promised.

Late that night, long after we had gone to bed, I awoke because my toes were itching like crazy. I turned on the light and noticed I had a lot of little bumps all over the toes of my right foot. I thought a giant spider had bitten me all over; one of my worst fears!

I ran into my mom's room to wake her up.

"Oh, no!" She exclaimed. "This looks like poison ivy! I told you kids not to play up in back!"

"I know, Mom, but we played there early today before you told us!"

"Oh, for Heaven's sake," sputtered Mom. "Now do not scratch or touch this at all!"

"But it itches so bad!" I complained.

"I'll put some calamine lotion on it so it won't itch."

"Well, hurry up—I can't stand it!"

Mom took cotton balls and dabbed the pink goop all over me. It helped for a few minutes, but then itched again.

"Don't scratch, Alicia Louise!" Mom warned. "You'll spread the poison ivy."

"It's hard not to, but I'll try," I promised.

I awoke the next morning itching twice as bad as the night before. As I entered Mom's room, I found her treating Billy all over his hands and fingers for the same wretched thing I had, only his had become huge blisters instead of tiny bumps.

"Oh, yours has spread, too," sighed Mom. "Grammy is bringing over some Phelsnaptha soap."

"What's that?" Billy asked.

"It's a soap that supposedly helps disinfect the poison in your skin so it won't spread anymore."

"I hope so!" Billy exclaimed.

Sure enough, Grammy came right over with a big bar of tan soap.

"Yuck!" I complained. "Mom, this smells terrible!"

"Just hang in there, Lishie," said Grammy. "It'll be over soon. This is how we always treated poison ivy through the years, although you usually have to wash it right away after you come in contact with the poison."

An hour later, we were both more itchy and miserable than ever. Billy's blisters were getting bigger and bigger. I noticed my little bumps were not so little anymore.

The next morning, I got up and almost fell over from a tight pain between my toes.

"Mom!" I screamed.

"What is it, Alicia?" Mom asked.

"Look at my foot!" I demanded.

"Oh, my gosh!"

I actually had webbed feet like a duck because my blisters had filled in the spaces between my toes. It made it difficult to walk.

Mom checked on Billy, who had also grown worse; his fingers were webbed like my toes! She went next door to the farmhouse to see Adele Brownlee who used to be a nurse. Mrs. Brownlee came right over to see us.

"It looks like Billy and Alicia are having an allergic reaction to the poison ivy. They should really see a doctor," she advised.

"I wasn't sure," admitted Mom. "Thank you so much, Adele!"

"Oh, you're quite welcome."

Mom called Dad and told him that we needed to go to the doctor.

"Karel, I'll come up early tomorrow morning so that we can get the kids in before the weekend."

"Oh, that would be great!" Mom's voice was full of relief. "I'll call around and make an appointment for them."

"Okay, I'll see you tomorrow around 10:00am."

"See you then, dear," said Mom.

Dad arrived early the next day.

"Well, I really should have sprayed the poison ivy last week. How are you doing, kids?" Dad asked.

"Not so good," I groaned.

"Well, Mom made an appointment for you two and we'll be leaving for Petoskey in a few minutes."

"Okay, Dad," said Billy.

We drove through Boyne City and then on to Petoskey where the doctor put us on dose packs, anti-toxins, to clear up the poison ivy. He also gave us a solution to soak in.

"What an ordeal this has turned out to be," sighed Mom. "Don't forget, we're having Bob and Louise Kennedy over tomorrow night."

"I haven't forgotten," assured Dad.

"We'll get some nice steaks to throw on the grill. Let's do hot dogs for the kids since they're not feeling well," suggested Mom. "That way they won't have to wait for a late dinner."

"Great idea!" Dad replied. "Why don't we have David come over to eat with the kids downstairs."

"They can play games and watch T.V.," agreed Mom.

Dad mixed up some medicine for us to soak our poison ivy in out on the deck so we wouldn't make a mess.

"I hate these blisters in between my toes. It makes it hard to walk!" I groaned.

"Well, you will be better soon enough, Sisterbell," said Dad in a very convincing voice.

Billy's hands were so swollen that he couldn't even use them to eat.

"Hello!" A voice from the distance said. It was Mrs. Brownlee. "How's the poison ivy coming?" She asked.

"Slowly but surely," said Dad.

"I hate these blisters," I told Mrs. Brownlee.

"Well, since you're soaking in medicine, we could sterilize a needle and drain the blisters," she said. "Then you could walk better, too!"

"Will it hurt?" I asked.

"Not at all," she assured me. "In fact, if you get me the needle, Karel, I can do it for her."

"You've got a deal!" Mom replied. She sterilized the needle and brought it to Mrs. Brownlee.

"I promise, you won't feel a thing!" Mrs. Brownlee said.

"I hope not!" I said with eyes squeezed shut.

"There," said Mrs. Brownlee.

"You mean it's all over?" I asked.

"Yes," she answered. "But, keep your foot up for about ten minutes so it drains properly and then put a Band-Aid on it."

"Thank you, Mrs. Brownlee!"

Mrs. Brownlee smiled. "You're welcome, Alicia."

After ten minutes or so, Dad came over and put a Band-Aid on me. "Now try to walk," he suggested.

"That's a lot better!" I said. "Now I can walk again without limping!"

"I wish you could drain my blisters," said Billy.

"Well, you have too many and I would be afraid of infection setting in. You'll be well in a few days," she said.

Mrs. Brownlee continued. "Well, I have to scoot. I'm going into Charlevoix to send some Murdick's fudge to my daughter, Dawn."

We all thanked Mrs. Brownlee for her help and she was on her way.

About ten minutes later, Billy was looking through the binoculars. "Hey! There's Mrs. Brownlee's car in line for the ferry. I can see her inside her car."

"Let me see, too!" I exclaimed.

Billy passed me the binoculars.

"You're right! I see her, too!"

We always had fun watching people on the ferry with the binoculars from home.

Mom and Dad were getting ready for the Kennedys to come over. Dad got the Webber grill all ready and then marinated the steaks before setting up a lot of glasses and drinks along with the ice bucket for cocktails.

All of the sliding glass doors were open and the sun glistened off the lake. There was enough of a breeze to make small ripples on the lake. Mom always said the deck is at its prettiest in the late afternoon until dusk.

"I put the little T.V. in Billy's room so that you kids can watch it if you want to," said Dad.

"Thanks Dad," I answered.

I looked down toward *Little Brown House* and saw David and his parents coming down the road. Dad greeted them at the door.

"Hello, Heins!" Mrs. Kennedy happily shouted.

"Hello, Louise, Robert, David," responded Dad.

Mom walked into the room from the deck and greeted everyone. "Why don't you kids go down to Billy's room so he doesn't get lonely? I'll bring your dinners down in a little bit."

"Okay!" We agreed and went downstairs to Billy's room. He was still stuck in bed because of his allergic reaction to severe poison ivy.

"Wow!" David said. "You've really got a bad case of poison ivy, don't you?"

"Yeah," answered Billy. "It's a real pain!"

"Oh, good," I said. "'Bewitched' is on T.V."

"It's not as good as this MAD Magazine I just got," replied Billy.

"Let me see," said David.

"Why do you boys like that dumb magazine?"

"You're the dummy!" Billy said. "It's a great magazine."

"Stop arguing," said Mom—as she walked into the room just then, and handed each of us a bottle of root beer and a basket with a hot dog and potato chips.

"Help your brother with his food, Alicia. His hands are too infected for him to touch his food."

"Okay, Mom, I will."

Mom returned upstairs.

"Here, Billy, open wide," I said. As Billy bit down on his hot dog, I quickly pulled it away.

"You'll have to bite quicker if you want to taste that," laughed David.

"Thanks a lot, Lish," said Billy.

"You want more?" I asked.

"What do you think?"

I put the hot dog in his mouth and kept pushing it. Billy started choking so I stopped immediately.

David was cracking up.

"My gosh!" Billy exclaimed. "What are you trying to do, kill me?"

David and I were laughing hysterically.

"What's so funny, David?" Billy asked.

"The ketchup and mustard you're wearing all over your face," David laughed.

"Well, what about your face?" Billy asked as he threw his root beer onto David's face. I, in turn, took a handful of potato chips and stuffed them down Billy's pajama top. David poured root beer onto Billy, but it hit me, too. We laughed uncontrollably!

"Do you kids want seconds?" Dad hollered from downstairs.

"Shhhhhh shhhhhh!" Billy hushed. But, we couldn't help it; we couldn't stop laughing! There was food everywhere except in our stomachs.

"I'm waiting," Dad reminded us.

"I'll come up and get some more in a minute, Dad!" I hollered back.

"Okay," Dad answered.

"C'mon, David, help me clean up this mess quickly!"

"Okay, okay."

We cleaned up the mess and then ate the rest of our food, watched T.V. and joked around until our parents were done socializing and David went home.

Within a week, all our poison ivy had disappeared…at least for this summer.

20 BROTHER BILLY'S FIRST YACHT

It was the middle of June and our fist summer in Deck-n-Dock was proving to be abundantly fun! This morning was sunny and bright.

"Good morning, Mommy," I said.

"Good morning, Sweetie," she answered. "You're a sleepy-head today."

As I sat up on the breakfast bar stool to eat, I heard pounding. "What's that?"

"Your brother is building something down on the beach."

I immediately got down from the stool to investigate.

"Just wait one minute there, Sister-bell!" Mommy scolded. "You finish your breakfast first."

"Oh, alright," I moaned.

As soon as I finished breakfast, I threw on some clothes and took off for the beach. I spotted Billy with Dad's toolbox, pounding away.

"What are you building?" I asked.

"A cabin cruiser!" Billy replied.

How exciting! I thought.

"Can I help?"

"Sure! You can be the First Mate."

So far, he had three logs, each about four feet long, tied and nailed together. Next, he nailed a piece of plywood over the logs, covering them. Then, he added several two-by-fours standing on each side. Finally, he secured one across the top, making it really look like a cabin cruiser.

It was time to launch her, so we put on our swimsuits.

"Mom! Come watch me launch my yacht!" Billy yelled to the house.

"Okay," Mom answered (hoping we wouldn't drown!)

"Get on, Lish," Billy ordered.

I did and then he gave it a huge push and jumped on board himself. You might guess what happened next; it was Christened "The S.O.S. Sinker!"

"Billy!" Mom yelled. "Get your sister off that sinking vessel and bring it back to shore."

"Okay Mom."

We played around with it for a few more days until Dad returned for the weekend.

"I'm sorry kids," he said upon inspecting it. "But, as of now, I am condemning this boat. The rusty nails and the fact that it doesn't float makes it a hazard."

So Daddy took an axe to the S.O.S. Sinker.

During the next week, Uncle Jim came driving down in front of Deck-n-Dock in his station wagon honking his horn. Billy, Mom and I ran down to greet him and saw an orange lifeboat protruding from the back of the station wagon. The letters on the side read "SPORTYAK."

"What's this?" Billy asked.

"It's an early birthday present, Billy," said Mom.

"Wow! You mean it's mine?"

"All yours!" Mom answered. "Uncle Jim ordered it from his marina."

"Thanks!" Billy said.

"It's an unsinkable two-seat lifeboat," said Uncle Jim.

Billy finally had a boat…and it floated!

21 A TRIP TO GRAYLING

One gloomy morning, Mommy was gathering a basket of what looked like craft items.

"What are you doing?" I asked.

"I'm going to Annabelle Webb's to work on a project," Mommy answered.

"Do you want to stay with Grammy or come with me?" Mommy asked. "Annabelle's granddaughter wants to meet you."

"Why didn't you say so in the first place?" I asked.

"You didn't give me a chance," Mommy replied.

"I'll come with you," I shouted anxiously.

As we went up Annabelle's steep driveway, her quaint yellow cottage was most welcoming. Annabelle greeted us with the friendliest of smiles.

"This is my granddaughter, Jill," she said.

"Hi!" I said to Jill.

"Hi!" She answered with a grin bigger than her grandmother's. She held out her hand and I went with her.

"My name is Jill."

"My name is Alicia."

"Let's go to my room," she suggested.

Jill had a cute little bedroom with lots of toys.

"This is my favorite," Jill said as she pulled down a clown doll dressed in blue. "His name is 'Cubby'."

"He's real cute," I said.

Jill giggled like I never heard anyone giggle before. Her giggle matched her continuous, happy grin. I liked her immediately, a genuine kindred spirit.

We enjoyed the day and made plans for the next day. I had so much fun with Jill and her grandmother that I started spending nights there, too.

Annabelle (Mrs. Webb) used to be a school teacher in Detroit. She had us do really fun projects, swimming in the afternoons and cooking lessons. Mrs. Webb's Chevy Caprice Classic was yellow and matched her cottage.

On our way to East Jordan one day she taught us a funny song, "Polly Wolly Doodle." Annabelle sang, "A grasshopper sat on a railroad track singing polly wolly doodle all the day, a-pickin' his teeth with a carpet tack, singing polly wolly doodle all the day! Fare thee well, farewell, fare thee well, farewell, fare thee well, my fairy fay, for I'm going to Louisiana for to see my Suzianna...singing polly wolly doodle all the day!" We sang, laughed and had a grand time!

I went home that night and Mommy asked me, "Would you like to go with Annabelle and Jill to Grayling for a week while they visit Annabelle's sister?"

"I sure would!" I exclaimed.

"I thought you would," Mom said. "Annabelle will be picking you up at 6:00 in the morning, so we need to pack you up and get you to bed early."

"Okay," I agreed with Mom.

Morning arrived and I was ready to go.

Annabelle and Jill came to our door.

"Greetings everyone!" Annabelle said.

"Thank you for inviting me, Mrs. Webb," I said.

"You are very welcome. We are so happy you can make the trip with us, aren't we, Jill?"

"Oh, yes, we are!" Jill said as she gave me a big hug and a huge smile. Jill's smile was again ear to ear – she was always happy!

As I hugged Mommy goodbye, she told me to have fun and to mind my manners.

"Karel, here is the phone number at my sister's house in Grayling."

"Thank you, Annabelle," Mom replied.

So, we left Hemingway Road and headed toward Grayling for a week full of fun and adventure. We played guessing games and sang songs along the way. The warm breeze coming through the car window was pleasant.

After about an hour, we stopped at a little diner for breakfast.

"How much longer before we get to Aunt Rosalynde's?" Jill asked.

"A little less than an hour," said Jill's grandma.

We had a great breakfast and started on our way again.

About a half-hour down the road, Annabelle pulled off the highway and onto a scenic two-lane road.

"I know where we are!" Jill exclaimed.

"Well, you should by now. You've been to Aunt Rosalynde's and Mary's many times," Annabelle said.

"Who's Mary?" I asked.

"Mary is Aunt Rosalynde's friend who lives with her. They have been friends for many years."

A few minutes later, we turned onto a dirt road, much like our Hemingway Road, but somewhat different. We then pulled into a dirt driveway in front of a huge pink two-story house.

"We're here," Annabelle announced.

Two elderly ladies came out of the front door.

Jill ran into one of the lady's arms and then the other's.

"Alicia, this is my sister, Rosalynde, and Mary," Annabelle said.

"How do you do?" I politely asked.

"Welcome, Alicia!" Rosalynde said, giving me a big hug. Mary did the same.

As we walked into their home, I was in awe of all the beautiful things that surrounded me, gorgeous furniture and knick-knacks. Then, I was really surprised to discover that this huge house came with two giant guest houses. They were also pink and matched the main house.

"Alicia, we get to stay in one of the guest houses," said Jill.

"We do?" I asked with excitement.

We got our luggage out of the car and took it to one of the guest houses. As we entered, I expected only sleeping quarters, but was delighted to find it to have a kitchen and living room. It was like being in a fancy hotel.

We unpacked and went to the main house for dinner. We sat in a beautiful dining room and had a very fancy dinner with several courses. I could see a body of water out of the dining room windows.

"What lake is that?" I asked.

"That is the Au Sable River," answered Rosalynde.

After dinner, we walked down to the river. It was much different than our Lake Charlevoix! It was very pretty, but the water was much darker and flowed rapidly in one direction.

"Why is the water moving one way like that?" I asked.

"That is the current," said Rosalynde.

"What's a current?" I asked.

"Well, it's like the wind or something strong under the water, pushing it hard in one direction," answered Annabelle.

"You girls can go swimming tomorrow," said Rosalynde.

As we walked back to our guest house, I noticed dozens of blue jays everywhere.

"Boy, there are a lot of blue jays here," I said.

As we walked toward our guest house, Rosalynde asked if I would like to see the other guest house. I nodded my head, 'yes.'

As we entered the other guest house, I couldn't believe what I was seeing. It was twice the size of the one we were staying in.

"This is very pretty!" I exclaimed.

"Thank you!" Rosalynde replied.

Rosalynde and Mary walked us back to our guest house. They said goodnight and headed back to the main house. We all got ready for bed and Annabelle turned out the lights. Jill and I giggled and talked until we fell asleep.

The next morning, we awoke to birds singing. I looked over at Jill, but she was still asleep. I looked for Annabelle, but did not see her.

"Good morning, Alicia," said Jill with another of her famous smiles.

"Good morning!" I answered. "Your grandma is gone."

"She's probably at the big house with Rosalynde and Mary."

So, we got dressed and headed for the big house. As we entered the main house, everyone was sitting at the table.

"Come in for breakfast, girls," invited Rosalynde.

We sat down to a scrumptious meal.

"May we go swimming?" Jill asked.

"Maybe this afternoon, we thought maybe you girls might like to go to the Fred Bear Museum."

Jill and I looked at each other and both nodded our heads, 'yes!'

After breakfast, we all piled into Rosalynde's blue-paneled Oldsmobile station wagon and headed for the museum. When we got there, we learned all about the big bears that live in the woods around Grayling and other parts of the country. There were big statues of all kinds of bears. There was a gift shop where I bought a little stuffed bear with money Mommy had given me for the trip. Jill also bought a souvenir.

It was a beautiful, sunny day. When we returned to the house, we changed into our bathing suits. The adults sat on beach chairs and watched as Jill and I entered the water. What a change from Lake Charlevoix! The minute I stepped into the water, I could feel the strong current. Every step deeper, I had to fight the current as it grew stronger. We only waded out into waist-deep water. There were other neighbors swimming, too. I saw some people on inner tubes going around in a circle. Later on, Rosalynde explained that those people were in a whirlpool on their inner tubes. How different, but exciting to swim in a river!

The next day, we went fishing and Rosalynde caught some beauties! She was a skilled fisher-lady and used very different tackle than what we used on Lake Charlevoix. We had so much fun that the days turned into minutes and soon it was time to leave and return to Hemingway Road.

In the short time we spent there, I had grown very fond of Rosalynde and Mary! I was sad to leave them. But, they promised to visit Hemingway Road very soon.

22 THE KENNEDYS' BREAKFAST GOODBYE

I couldn't believe it, but my summer with David had quickly come to an end. The Kennedys were going back to Dixon, Illinois for the year. What would I do without my Hemingway Road companion? I suppose all good things eventually had to come to a close. David had told me for a week they were leaving, but I stubbornly put it out of my head until I no longer could.

It was still dark one Sunday morning when I heard Mom and Dad stirring upstairs. I smelled coffee and food cooking, but I did not want to go upstairs because I would have to accept the inevitable – my good summer friend was going home. I finally decided to get dressed and say goodbye.

As I came upstairs, I saw that my mom had put the leaf in the dining room table and had set it beautifully. Billy was already up and was on the beach wiping out his Sportyak from the morning dew.

The Kennedys arrived as the sun began to shine through the sliding glass doors. Mrs. Kennedy was carrying a big wicker basket full of their leftovers that they could not take with them. David, his parents, Albie and Louie sat down at the table. Billy followed them. Everyone was talking as food was passed around the table. I was in my own silent world as I knew that we would not see these kind people for almost a year.

"Our handyman will be out to close up the cottage in about a week," said Mr. Kennedy.

"Always so much to do in the opening or closing of the cottages," replied

Dad.

"Yes, that seems to be the case," agreed Mr. Kennedy.

Billy and David were conversing; in fact, the whole table was alive with chatter. I looked out onto the lake. Boats were out and the sun was shining brightly as it reflected off the water. It just didn't seem right that anyone had to leave Hemingway Road when summer was still in its prime. Soon, everyone was finished.

"Well, I suppose it's time to get started," said Mrs. Kennedy.

Billy and David shook hands and clowned around while they said their goodbyes. I felt like I could burst into tears, but somehow managed to hold them back.

"Goodbye David. See you next summer," I said.

"Yeah, see ya!" He replied. His still-sunburned face would be missed!

Everyone said goodbye and the Kennedys walked back to their cottage.

Mom, Dad and Grammy started cleaning up. I stood by the sliding glass door and sobbed quietly as I watched the Kennedys until they were out of sight.

Dad came over to me and said, "Don't cry. You'll see them next year! Besides, now I can spend some time fishing with you."

"That sounds like fun," I said eagerly.

"Just give me an hour to help Mom and we'll be off."

"Okay Dad."

I walked down to our beach and skipped a few stones before I went down to check the mail, as it was a chore.

As I passed the Kennedys', the cottage still looked open and friendly. I walked up their driveway and noticed the two big garage doors were padlocked shut. For a moment, I thought I could smell Coppertone suntan lotion, which was always in abundance during their stay as they were all very fair-skinned. I walked around the corner and saw the icehouse doors also locked. We had been in and out of those Dutch doors dozens of times over the last month. I decided to leave before I felt sad again.

Goodbye, my good friend David, until next summer.

23 LABOR DAY WEEKEND ARRIVES

The last twelve weeks had been the most joyous of my young life! The newness of Deck-n-Dock, swimming lessons (those were scary but with Sheila, they were okay), seeing my good friend David Kennedy, being in the Venetian Festival Parade, collecting Petoskey stones, finding worn glass on walks to Hemingway Point with Grammy, picking endless amounts of daisies, going on walks in the old Hemingway Nursery, visiting with all our neighbors along Hemingway Road, smelling the smoke of everyone's chimney on the few cold days we had, going fishing, riding the Ironton Ferry, picking wild strawberries and raspberries, long rides in Uncle Jim and Aunt Maxine's cabin cruiser, learning and loving the nature that surrounded me, are locked in my memory forever.

Our first summer season on Hemingway Road was over. Dad came up on Friday night, as usual, but things were not the same. Saturday morning, the people from Bay Marina were taking our dock down. They piled up the dock pieces one on top of the other on the beach. Later in the afternoon, Uncle Jim and Scott came over to Deck-n-Dock. Uncle Jim and Dad carried down the blinds for *Little Brown House* and boarded up the windows. *Little Brown House* was so dark inside afterward! All the screens across the front porch were boarded up just like the Kennedys. It was so sad that I returned to Deck-n-Dock.

Mom was stripping all the beds and packing all the sheets and blankets in plastic bags.

"Why are you putting everything in plastic bags?" I asked.

"Well, just in case some mice or other rodents try to get in, if everything is wrapped, it will be more protected."

As I looked through Deck-n-Dock, everything had changed. The yellow refrigerator and freezer were empty and propped open by a broom.

I heard noises on the deck. Uncle Jim and Dad were taking our redwood furniture and Webber grill inside the bathhouse. I looked out onto the lake and saw no boats. Everything was quiet; too quiet.

I longed for a mid-July day with an abundance of boat activity on the lake. It was breezy and the wind was cool. It was even too cold to go for a last swim of the season. I looked over toward the ferry and it was stopped on the other side of the lake. I couldn't even hear the "chug-a chug" one more time. Mom had deflated and put all the beach toys in the big red laundry basket. Uncle Jim and Scott said goodbye and returned to Charlevoix and the rest of their family.

Grammy came up to Deck-n-Dock. I looked over at *Little Brown House*. It looked so sad being boarded up. I wouldn't be going in the screen door tomorrow morning. I will be back at our winter home.

As we all stood in the living room of Deck-n-Dock, Mom pulled all of the curtains closed across the front of the cottage. As we exited, Deck-n-Dock looked dark and lonely already. Dad locked the door, Grammy, Mom, and Billy got into the station wagon. Dad pulled out first and then Mom followed.

"What's the matter?" Dad asked.

"I don't want to leave!" I said with a tear rolling down my cheek.

"We'll be back before you know it!" Dad said, trying to console me.

We went down the big hill by the Bull's and Hargraves'. As we passed by their mailboxes, I realized that none of them would be opened for at least ten months. It was a dark day and white caps were big on the lake, almost like the lake knew that summer was over.

As we drove by all the cottages, all the docks were down and the windows were boarded up. There was no sign of life, because we were the last to leave Hemingway Road. I took my last glance at the lake as we approached Ferry Road.

Goodbye Hemingway Road. See you next summer.

24 THE "MOREL" OF THE STORY

The winter months were long and cold, but school would be out in another
three weeks for vacation. This past spring, we had moved to Jackson,
Michigan, as Dad had been promoted to be the manager of the Jackson
Citizen Patriot. Summer was almost here; the spring was slow in coming,
but flowers were in bloom as I looked out my classroom window at Trinity
Lutheran School. I was especially excited because after school, we wouldn't
be going home – we were going to Deck-n-Dock and Hemingway Road.

Mom and Dad picked us up with a loaded station wagon. It was a beautiful day for the trip.

"We're making such good time, I think we'll skip Mt. Pleasant for dinner and go onto Gaylord," said Dad.

"I'm not hungry at all yet," Mom said.

"How about you kids," asked Dad.

"We're not hungry either," we both said.

"Great!" Dad said. "This will allow us to beat the Memorial Day weekend traffic."

We arrived in Gaylord at 6:30pm. There stood the huge statue of Paul Bunyan across the street from the Holiday Inn where we often ate. Dinner was good as usual and we only had an hour or so left until we arrived in Charlevoix.

"Okay, kids, we're in Boyne City and there's the first view of Lake Charlevoix."

"Yeah!" We yelled.

Even though it was dark, the lights reflecting off the water gave us a good glimpse of our lake. We drove around Lake Charlevoix and then through a little town called Advance.

All of a sudden, Dad slammed on the brakes yelling, "Hang on!" Three beautiful deer had run out in front of us on the road.

"Oh, they're so pretty," I said.

"I better slow down a bit," Dad said.

"Yes, you better," said Mommy.

"The deer are not used to any traffic along the road yet this year," Daddy explained.

A few minutes later, Dad slowed down and we turned onto Hemingway Road. We turned up the big hill and arrived at Deck-n-Dock. Dad unlocked the front door and turned on the spotlights so that we could see.

As usual, the spider webs were abundant.

Tomorrow would be great because the cousins would be over and life on Hemingway Road would come alive once again. Besides getting the cottages open and ready for our second summer of enjoyment, there were always many things to check on and explore for another summer season. For instance, we would see if the shoreline was up or down from last year or we would check on the playhouse to see how it weathered the winter.

Grammy taught us to check on two other items during the years during Memorial Day weekend: wild asparagus and morel mushrooms. You could spot the morels almost anywhere, at the base of trees or just in the middle of the yard. However, Grammy, being up on Hemingway Road for many years, knew of all the best places to find morels and asparagus. There is one place up in the old Hemingway Tree Farm where both morels and asparagus grow in abundance, side by side. Unbelievably, it is "the dump." All the way around the outside of the dump you could find very large morels and in the field next to the dump was filled with wild asparagus.

Memorial Day weekend was not quite the same as a vacation weekend. This was the "weekend for work!" *Little Brown House* and Deck-n-Dock had been closed up for the winter and this was the weekend to re-open them. There was a tremendous amount of dusting, vacuuming, window cleaning, and cobweb removing. We would pull the patio, deck and porch furniture from storage and put out the dock. Sheila, Stephen and I were still small enough to get away without too many chores during this work weekend. We quickly learned that it was much better to stay out of the way than to get caught up in all the chaos of cleaning.

"Well, I hope Mr. Donaldson remembered to have the electricity turned on today!" Mom exclaimed.

"I'm sure he did," Dad replied. "He's never let us down, yet."

As we arrived at Deck-n-Dock, it had that "closed up" smell.

"Take your luggage downstairs," Mom said.

"I'm not going down there until Dad sprays bug spray in my room!" I exclaimed.

"Alright," Dad agreed.

"Make sure you check for spiders, Dad," I instructed.

"Oh, I will, 'Miss Spider Lady," he chuckled.

As I snuggled under the covers that night, I was glad that any bug in my room had now been exterminated. Even though my room smelled of bug spray, it was worth it!

A few minutes later, I was startled to hear the "huff puff puff" of the furnace turning on. Half of my closet was for clothes and the other half contained the loudest furnace you ever heard. There was another sound I heard after the furnace turned off. It was a very welcome sound, that of the waves hitting the shoreline. It always put me to sleep.

I awoke to the smell of coffee and the sound of my parents talking upstairs. I looked out my sliding glass door to see sunshine and white caps on the lake. What a beautiful sight! I got dressed and went upstairs for breakfast.

"When are the cousins coming over?" I asked.

"Any time now," Dad answered.

"Yeah!" I gleefully shouted.

Just then, I looked down toward *Little Brown House* and saw the cousins going into the house. Down off my stool I slid!

"Bye Lishie," Mom smiled.

"Goodbye, my cousins are here," I explained.

"Shut that screen door, Alicia Louise!"

"Okay."

After many hugs and kisses, Sheila and I took off. We ran down to Grammy's beach to stand on the fireplace.

"Don't you girls go off too far," reminded Aunt Maxine.

After a few minutes, Grammy was rinsing some mop water out into her yard.

"Hey," I said. "Let's ask Grammy if she'll take us up in the nursery to look for morels and asparagus!"

"Okay," Sheila agreed.

"Grammy, will you take us to look for morels and asparagus later?"

"Girls, we have lots of work to do. But, if you let us get most of our work done, I'll take you after lunch."

"We will!"

After lunch, Grammy took us up behind *Little Brown House*.

"We don't have time to go to the nursery, but I'm sure we'll find some morels right here. Just look under the big trees."

Just then, Grammy leaned over and picked up two huge morel mushrooms. We scrambled all over and each found a few more mushrooms.

"There are more up by the dump," Grammy said. "We'll go sometime this weekend."

"Aw, we want to go now."

"Well, there's too much work to do," Grammy said. "We'll go later on this weekend." Grammy then said she had to go back inside and continue working. She took the mushrooms we found and soaked them in salt water to get the dirt out. Grammy said that the morels tasted like steak.

Sheila and I looked for something to do. While looking in Grammy's garage, we saw the red greyhound wagon that had been moved to *Little Brown House*.

"Let's play with the wagon," said Sheila.

"Alright," I agreed. "Let's go up to the dump to look for morels and asparagus."

"We're not supposed to go too far away," she reminded me.

"I know, but the dump is not far at all," I reasoned. "Let's take the wagon to put morels and asparagus in."

We made our way to the nursery and to the dump. The dump was a big hole filled with years of Hemingway Road garbage. We each took a side to find big mushrooms and then got together to compare the sizes. After we couldn't find any more mushrooms, we started to the field next to the dump to look for asparagus. We found tons of it!

"Remember, Grammy said to find the thin stalks because they are more tender," I said.

"Yeah, but the big ones look better," said Sheila.

The wagon was filling up with mushrooms and asparagus.

"Grammy will be really surprised, won't she?" Sheila asked.

"Oh, I think this will be the most asparagus and morels that she's ever gotten."

Back at Deck-n-Dock, Uncle Jim hollered up from *Little Brown House*, "Hey, are you guys having fun yet?"

"Oh, loads," laughed Mom from the deck. "Why don't you guys all come up here for a coffee break?"

"We'll be right up!"

"Bill, help me put some coffee and refreshments on, please," said Mom.

"I'm a step ahead of you," he replied.

"Since the deck furniture is out, let's have coffee on the deck," Mom suggested. "Thanks for all your hard work, Billy."

"You're welcome," he answered. "Shelly and Scott have been working hard, too."

"Lish and Sheila are getting away with murder," said Scott as he entered the deck.

"I know," said Billy.

"Hey," said Shelly. "They're staying out of the way of progress." Everyone, including our parents laughed.

"Where are they?" Mom asked.

"I haven't seen them in a couple of hours," Maxine replied.

"They'll turn up soon," said Uncle Jim.

Sheila and I were very proud of our amount of goods as we pulled the wagon toward home. We stood at the top of the nursery hill leading down directly to the cottages. To the right of us was the dry fountain, a reminder of the old Hemingway Tree Farm.

"This fountain must have been so pretty when the nursery was open," I said.

"It's pretty without water and weeds growing in and all around it," said Sheila.

I felt sad that such a pretty fountain was dry and abandoned.

"Well," said Sheila. "Do you want to take the wagon down, or should I?"

"I've been thinking it might be easier for us to ride in it."

The steep and narrow path had no wall or fence protecting it.

"As long as it's better than our trip down to Lake Michigan last Christmas!" Sheila exclaimed.

"Of course it will be better," I promised. "This is not ice and snow."

"You steer!" Sheila shouted.

So, I sat in the front by the handle to steer and Sheila sat Indian-style in the back and we were ready to roll. I pushed off with my feet. The wagon went much faster than the blue boat at Christmas! We both screamed at the top of our lungs.

"That's the girls," yelled Aunt Maxine.

Our parents, brothers and Shelley came running toward us.

"Oh, my gosh," Mom yelled. "They're going to go over the side."

Just then, we hit a half-buried rock and almost flipped over. I felt unbelievable fear! The handle in my hands was out of control and fighting me.

We finally reached the bottom of the hill and slipped through Uncle Jim's hands. Dad was right behind Uncle Jim and he caught us. After we were hugged dearly, we were sentenced to sit on the deck stairs until told differently.

"Gee, we didn't get to give Grammy the asparagus and morels," I said sorrowfully.

"Well, I hate to tell you, Lish, but most of them went flying out on our trip down!"

"Oh, drats!" I said. "Well, after our punishment, we can go look for them."

"If I know our parents, a bath and bed will be our next move," said Sheila.

"You're right," I moaned. "Well, Sheila, the moral of this story is that we should stay away from all modes of transportation down steep hills!"

"You said it, Lish!" Sheila exclaimed.

25 "HEINSITE"

There was really only one thing missing from Deck-n-Dock...a boat! Mom and Dad decided to get one from home where we lived during the winter months. It was about a four and a half hour trip between our winter home and Charlevoix. Mom and Dad picked out a cute motorboat. It was olive green and matched the color of Deck-n-Dock. The big motor on the back of the boat read "Johnson 33" and a picture of a seahorse was also on the motor. It was Friday and we were ready to tow the boat behind our Chevrolet Nova station wagon up to Hemingway Road. Dad seemed a little nervous. The weather could have cooperated more; it was very windy! Dad had us all look behind the boat a million times, especially Mom. Her neck started to get a crick in it. Mom was not into sports or boats.

"Karel, could you check again?"

"I hope it isn't there when I turn around," she said. "I never want to do this again!"

"We should have bought our boat up in Charlevoix and saved ourselves more than the money we saved back home," he said. "This is a pain in the neck."

"You're not kidding," Mom agreed.

As we arrived on Hemingway Road, I almost heard Mom and Dad sigh with relief that we were finally there and the wretched boat-hauling trip was over. Instead of going up the hill to our garage, Dad pulled the boat up in front of Deck-n-Dock. Dad had ordered a shore station the week before and had Bay Marina put it in the water alongside our dock. It looked like a big square with a giant wheel to hoist the boat out of the water.

"When can we put the boat in the water?" I asked.

"On Tuesday," Dad answered. "I'm going to take it to Uncle Jim's marina to launch it. It will be easier with the boat launch."

We couldn't wait to get our new boat into the water!

After dinner, we were all sitting in the living room watching T.V.

"Mom?" I asked. "What are we going to name our boat?"

"I never thought of giving it a name," she exclaimed.

"What about Deck-n-Dock 2?" Billy asked.

"What about Heinsite?" Mom suggested.

"What a great name!" Dad exclaimed.

"Yeah!" Billy and I both shouted.

"So Heinsite it is!" Dad said.

Tuesday morning came quickly and Mom and Dad drove the boat to Uncle Jim's marina. The shore station was already waiting in the water next to the dock for Heinsite. Mom and Dad stayed on the shore while Uncle Jim launched Heinsite.

As he started the motor, he began to steer the boat in a crazy way.

"What's wrong?" Mom asked.

"I don't know," Dad replied.

Just then, Uncle Jim yelled out, "The steering cables are backwards."

"Oh, my gosh," Mom exclaimed.

"It's okay, Karel," said Dad. "Jim will handle it. If anyone can handle a backwards boat, it's Jim."

Jim finally got it under control and fixed the steering so it worked correctly. Uncle Jim unhooked the trailer from our station wagon so Mom could drive home easily.

Dad went home by Lake Charlevoix with Uncle Jim. We heard the boat and met Dad and Uncle Jim as they hoisted Heinsite up on the shore station for the first time. Our green and white boat matched our green Deck-n-Dock. We looked forward to a lot of fun times on Heinsite!

26 THE COWBELL AND THE SIREN

We were up on Hemingway Road for our second summer. We drove both cars up again on a Friday afternoon, June 19. The next day was Mom's birthday. We settled in all day Saturday and then Dad took us all into Charlevoix to Grey Gables for their famous whitefish to celebrate Mom's birthday. There was a man named Breezy who sang for our entertainment.

Sunday went fast and Dad had to head back to Jackson for a week of work. We kissed him goodbye and couldn't wait until he arrived back on Friday.

"We will meet you at the end of the road on Friday," I told Dad.

"Okay, see you then," he replied before driving off.

Grammy came over for dinner and we ate on the deck to celebrate our first night's dinner at Deck-n-Dock that summer. All of a sudden, a loud siren went off. Grammy almost dropped her fork.

"What in tarnation is that?" Mom asked.

"It sounds like a fire engine," said Grammy.

"Let's take a walk down the road to see what's going on," suggested Mom. We walked past the mailboxes and did not yet see anything wrong or hear the siren again. We were in front of the Newmans' and Harkness' cottages. Mr. And Mrs. Harkness were sitting on their front porch.

"Hello Mrs. Shepard," said Mrs. Harkness.

"Why hello," Grammy answered. "Did you hear a loud siren?"

"Oh, yes!" Mrs. Harkness exclaimed. "I'm sorry if it alarmed you. My daughter, Joan, uses it to call her children home for dinner."

"What a good idea!" Mom said.

"It's hard to call kids home with them going off in all different directions," Mrs. Harkness explained. She had three grandchildren, Mike, Denise and Barbie.

"Well, we're glad nothing's wrong," said Grammy. "Now we'll know it's dinner time when the siren goes off. May we come for dinner, too?" Grammy joked.

"Anytime, Mrs. Shepard," said Mrs. Harkness with a smile. "We'll see you later on."

"Goodbye."

Later that week, Mom drove us all into East Jordan to Huckle's Antiques, one of Mom's and Grammy's favorite hangouts. Mom bought a big cowbell on a leather strap.

"What's that for?" I asked.

"Well, you know why the Newmans have the siren, right?"

"Yes."

"This will be the way I call you and Billy home from now on so that you can hear me."

I jiggled the cowbell and it was loud, alright.

The next day, Mom wanted us home for dinner and rang the cowbell. A few minutes later, the siren went off.

"My goodness," exclaimed Grammy. "It sounds like a cow summoned the police!"

We all laughed.

27 RAINY DAYS ON HEMINGWAY ROAD

Unfortunately, on occasion, it would rain on Hemingway Road. One morning, I awoke to more darkness in my room than I was used to. I got dressed and went upstairs for breakfast.

"No swimming today," Mom said.

"Maybe it will stop raining," I said optimistically.

"I don't think so."

"How do you know, Mom?"

"Well, I have spent many summers on Hemingway Road and I know when the lake is very calm like this, it rains all day long," she explained.

"I see Grammy on her front porch. I'm going to go visit her and see what she thinks about the rain," I said, wanting a second opinion.

"Okay," Mom said. "Be careful going down the stairs. They're slippery."

I carefully went down the steps toward *Little Brown House* and walked up the two wide steps to the screen door. As I pushed open the door, it made its usual squeaky sound and then slammed closed.

"Hello Lishie," said Grammy. "Come sit down with me. Would you like some juice?"

"No thank you. I just had breakfast," I answered. "Grammy? Do you think it will rain all day?"

"Well, I suppose from the looks of this, it will be an all-day sizzle-sozzle."

"Sizzle-sozzle?"

"An all-day quiet but steady rain," she explained.

Just then, I saw David walking down the road toward Deck-n-Dock.

"David! Wait up!" I shouted. "Bye Grammy."

"Bye Lishie."

I met up with David and we went up to Deck-n-Dock. We have an entire drawer full of rainy-day games, puzzles and comic books. David and I were playing magnetic Tic-Tac-Toe when the phone rang. Mom answered it. A few minutes later, she said, "That was Louise (David's mother). She has invited you over for lunch."

"C'mon, David. Let's go."

"You kids take the back path behind the Brown house so that you don't get too wet," said Mom.

"Okay," we both answered.

As we scurried down the stairs and over toward the back path, it was all very still outside. Beside the sound of a steady light rain, the only other sound was the "chug-a chug-a-chug" of the Ironton Ferry. It was cool and damp and I could smell smoke coming from the chimney of *Little Brown House*. Grammy loved the little potbellied stove in her kitchen. Every time I used the back path, I would stop and pick a fresh chive from Grammy's garden. The mild onion flavor was refreshing.

As we approached David's cottage, we went into the back kitchen door. Their cottage had a back utility room just like *Little Brown House* did, except there was an old-fashioned washing machine in their back room. We entered the big kitchen.

"Oh, good," David said. "Rice-a-Roni."

"It will be ready in a few minutes," said David's mom. "Hello Alicia."

"Hi Mrs. Kennedy."

We sat at the table on their big front porch. It was a built-in porch with lots of windows across the front of it. The view of their beach and Lake Charlevoix was beautiful.

David's mom put a plate down in front of both of us.

"Thank you."

"You're quite welcome, Alicia."

I loved their plates because they were all different colors. David got a dark blue plate and I got a yellow plate. Mom said it was called Fiesta Ware. Grammy had a few pieces too, but not as many as the Kennedys.

"Where are your brother and sister?" I asked.

"Probably upstairs in their rooms reading or something," said David. Albie and Louie were teenagers.

"We could go spy on them for something to do," said David.

"That sounds fun," I replied.

We went through the living room and crept up the stairs.

"Shhh," This is Louie's room," said David. The door was slightly ajar. David leaned in and then back.

"Now, you!" He instructed.

I leaned in and saw Louie reading a book on her bed. Over on her dresser was the collection of Indian dolls I always admired. David pulled me back and then leaned back in. I giggled and pushed him into her room.

"Hello David," said Louie. "Are you quite done now? Why don't you bother Albie? He would probably like it."

"Yeah, we were thinking about it," said David.

"Okay," said Louie. "I'm going to get back to my book."

We went toward Albie's room. The door was completely closed. David bent down and looked through the keyhole.

"Hmmm, I don't see him," said David.

Just then, Albie snuck up behind us and roared like a lion, startling us!

"What do you think you guys are up to?" Albie asked.

"Not a whole lot," said David.

"How are you Alicia?" Albie asked.

"Fine," I answered.

"Let's go down to the icehouse," suggested David.

"Okay."

The icehouse was just that. Years ago, it was used to keep ice cool during the summer. It was now used to store the Kennedy's picnic table and beach furniture during the winter. As we opened the double door and entered the ice house, I was wary of spiders. There were a few old chairs and an even older Victrola in the icehouse. It still worked. The icehouse had an odor all its own. It was kind of musty, but I liked it because nothing else smelled the way the icehouse did, which made it a special smell. I could just picture it filled with ice covered with saw dust in the older days.

The icehouse was our summer hang-out during rainy days. We could spend endless hours talking and goofing off. Then it was getting late and I had to be getting home.

"Let's go fishing tomorrow," said David.

"Okay. Bright and early while the fish are still biting."

"See you tomorrow."

"See ya!"

28 ANCHORS AWAY!

It was another glorious summer day on Hemingway Road. It was a Sunday afternoon and we had been to church in Petoskey and now had returned to Deck-n-Dock for an afternoon of lakefront fun. We had just finished lunch when Grammy called up from her yard, "Karel, Bill! Jim called and he's bringing the family out on the Blue Max for a swim later on."

"Great!" Dad responded. "We'll look forward to it."

Later that day, Mom, Dad, Grammy, Billy and I were relaxing on the beach when we heard the sound of the Blue Max humming. The spray in front of the bow was brisk. Then the boat slowed down. The Blue Max bounced gracefully in front of our dock. The whitecaps on the lake were beautiful, but rough. Uncle Jim pulled the Blue Max up to the dock. Since the wind was strong, he anchored the boat instead of tying it to the dock. We were all having a great time swimming, playing in the sand and skipping stones. Mom and Grammy made refreshments. Sheila and I picked endless daisies as we always did. The afternoon was perfect! I was also excited because Uncle Tom ("U.T.") and Aunt Glenna were arriving from Rockford, Michigan this afternoon. It was fun out in the water with the rafts and inner tubes since the waves were getting bigger.

Grammy passed around some of her famous oatmeal cookies. Just then we heard some car doors slam behind *Little Brown House*. It was Aunt Glenna and Uncle Tom.

"Put on your suits and come down to the beach!" Grammy called to them. "You can unpack later!"

Uncle Tom walked right off the end of the dock and into the water.

"Come on, Glenna," said Tom. "Jump in!"

"That's okay," she replied. "I'll wade in later."

"Chicken!" Uncle Tom joked.

The rest of us were playing and swimming. Scott, Billy and Shelley were diving off the end of the dock.

"Jim?" Aunt Maxine asked. "I think the boat is drifting a bit."

"It sure is!" He exclaimed. "The wind is getting stronger and the anchor is dragging along the bottom. I'll swim out to the boat to fix it."

He climbed aboard Blue Max and just then, the rope from the boat pulled tightly across the side of the dock.

Uncle Tom yelled to Shelley and Billy who were standing on the end of the dock, "JUMP!" They did, right at the moment the entire dock fell into the lake.

Uncle Jim grabbed the anchor line and untied it, but it was too late. Dad and Uncle Tom jumped into the lake to retrieve dock parts. Uncle Jim started Blue Max and yelled out, "I'm going to have to tie it up across the lake at Scott's. It's getting too rough."

"I'll drive over to the ferry to pick you up," said Mom.

Uncle Tom, Dad, Billy and Scott picked up most of the dock pieces by the time Mom and Uncle Jim returned.

"Did you get the boat tied up alright?" Grammy asked.

"Yeah," replied Uncle Jim. "But, they're pretty crowded over there, so we have to get going."

"I'll run you back over," said Dad.

"We'll get that dock back up this week," said Uncle Jim.

"Don't worry," said Dad. "I'll have the marina put it up."

"I lost my anchor," said Uncle Jim.

"Billy," said Uncle Jim. "I'll give you a reward if you find my anchor."

"Okay," said Billy.

We said goodbye to the cousins as they headed back to Charlevoix. I was always sad anytime the cousins had to leave, even though they lived nearby in Charlevoix.

About fifteen minutes later, the Blue Max came by Hemingway Road and we all waved goodbye. I watched the Blue Max until it was out of sight.

29 THE PLAYHOUSE

One afternoon, we were visiting Margaret and Homer at Birchmont. Margaret was telling us about the little log cabin up behind Birchmont that used to be up in the Hemingway Tree Farm used for her father George's first office. He later built a large office and had the little log cabin moved down behind Birchmont.

"You know, our kids, Joan and Jay, used the little log cabin as a playhouse," said Margaret. "How would you children like to use it for your playhouse?"

"We would love it!" I exclaimed.

"I'll unlock it so you can get in. Just make sure you keep the door shut when you leave," said Homer.

"We will!" Billy promised.

"I'll give a set of keys to your parents so that you can use it even after we return to Arizona."

"Thank you!" We both said.

When we got to the playhouse that afternoon, it was exciting to know we could have access to such a neat place! There was a nice covered porch across the front. Billy painted a sign that read, "The Playhouse" and painted a few seagulls on the sign. We swept out all the cobwebs and opened the windows to air it out. The musty smell seemed to be permanent. We put flowers in the flower box outside the window. There was an old rocking chair and a cane seat chair plus a little table inside the cabin. There were also some old dishes and old milk bottles on the table. We worked, cleaned and fixed until we thought we had created a "dream house." Now, we would have a fun place to go when the cousins came over. There was a crab-apple tree in the front yard. Lilac bushes surrounded the playhouse. The apple orchard was up the hill from the playhouse. Grammy found a little rug we could have for our new playhouse. The playhouse would become part of all our summers on Hemingway Road.

30 A BOAT TRIP WITH HOMER

It was another pretty day as Billy and I walked over to see Margaret and Homer.

"Come in, come in children," said Homer as he held open the screen door. We sat on their screened porch.

"Good morning dear children," said Margaret.

"Say, would you children like to take a ride into Charlevoix by boat with me this afternoon?" Homer asked.

"Oh, yes!" We both shouted.

"Be sure to ask your mother's permission," said Homer.

"We will," answered Billy.

"Well, that's fine," said Homer.

"Are you coming, Margaret?" I asked.

"Oh, Heavens, no!" Margaret laughed. "I don't ride in the boat. It messes up my hair!"

We visited for a while and then returned home.

"You children be back here at 1:00p.m. for our boat ride," reminded

Homer.

"Okay," Billy replied.

We asked Mom if we could go with Homer. She said we could as long as we both wore life jackets. We agreed. We ate lunch and then headed back to Birchmont. Homer was on the dock.

"We're almost ready to go," he said. He was lowering the boat so that we could get into it easier. Homer's boat was a pretty red and white one.

"You children go ahead and get in and I'll lower the boat the rest of the way."

Homer got in, too.

"Billy, you be the captain!" Homer said.

"Aye aye, sir!" Billy agreed.

The lake was a beautiful blue that day. I sat in the back and was ready to enjoy a pleasant trip to Charlevoix. Billy backed out and we were on our way. As we got into the big part of the lake, the water became a little choppier. I liked to put my arm over the side of the boat to feel the cool spray of water that was kicked up by our speed. We passed Sequionota to the left where we would often anchor to go swimming because there was sand at the bottom of the lake there. As other boaters passed by, I cheerfully waved to them. Margaret was right. The wind does mess up your hair, but I loved every minute of it. A big cabin cruiser passed by and we rode the waves gracefully.

The water got calmer as we approached the railroad bridge and Round Lake. Several boats were entering the beautiful harbor.

"Head over to the municipal docks," said Homer.

Billy found an empty slip and pulled up to it. Homer tied the boat to the dock.

"Excellent job, Billy!" Homer replied.

"Thanks," said Billy.

Homer needed to go to the hardware store and then a little market that faced Round Lake. We walked past the trout pond. It was filled with both German Brown Trout and Rainbow Trout. Homer handed us each a penny with which to make a wish and toss into the trout pond. He made a purchase at the hardware store and then we went on to the market. He asked us both to pick out a piece of candy. I picked a "Pink Owl" bubble gum cigar.

"Thank you, Homer," I said.

"You're very welcome."

I was going to chew it on the way back to Hemingway Road. As we started back, I saw the bridge open for a big sailboat. I opened my cigar bubble gum and put the label on my finger like a ring. I figured that I would take a bite every five minutes so that it would last all the way to Ironton. Homer and Billy were busy talking. We arrived back to the cottage in about twenty-five minutes. I took my last bite as Billy docked the boat. Homer got out first and then rose the boat up to dock level. He held out his hand and helped me out of the boat.

"Thank you, Homer, for the fun afternoon," I said happily.

"You're welcome, Alicia," he replied. Homer always pronounced my name "Aleesha" instead of "Alisha."

I skipped all the way home to tell Mom and Grammy about our nice trip. It is my job to report to Mom before Billy ever got a chance. What are little sisters for?

31 MY SPECIAL BIRTHDAY DINNER

This year, for my birthday, Mom invited our cousins, Aunt Maxine and Uncle Jim and Grammy for dinner on the beach. I was so happy because my birthday fell on a Friday night and my Dad was able to make it on time for dinner. Mom made my favorite Devil's food marshmallow sheet cake.

While we were having dinner, Margaret and Homer were taking an evening stroll and stopped by to say 'hello.'

"Today is my birthday," I told them.

"Well, happy birthday, Alicia!" They both said.

They continued their walk and my wonderful party came to an end. I took a shower and went upstairs for a while.

"Who was that on the phone?" I asked.

"Margaret called," said Mom. "She and Homer have invited you out to dinner at the Grey Gables in Charlevoix tomorrow night for your birthday present."

"Wow! That would be fun!" I exclaimed.

"They want you to go over to Birchmont at 5:00p.m. tomorrow night," said Mom.

Saturday arrived and I had my usual fun swimming and enjoying the beach.

"It's 4:00p.m., Alicia, come up to get ready for your dinner party," Mom called to me.

"Okay," I answered. "I'll be right up!"

I got dressed up in my flowered linen dress Mom had made for me. I wore lacy white knee socks and my patent leather shoes.

"You look very pretty!" Dad said.

"Be polite and have a good time," instructed Mom.

"I will," I promised. "Bye!"

When I got to Birchmont, Margaret and Homer were waiting for me on the front porch.

"Come in!" Homer said.

"You look so nice," complimented Margaret.

"Thank you."

Margaret and Homer were dressed up, too. We got into their car and headed to the Ironton Ferry for the trip to Charlevoix. About twenty minutes later, we were at the Grey Gables.

The Grey Gables is a fancy restaurant in a beautiful old house. As we entered, music was playing. We sat down at our table and were handed menus.

"Do you need help reading the menu, dear?" Margaret asked.

"No," I answered. "I always have the white fish when I come here."

"I believe that is what I'll have, too," said Margaret.

"Well, that makes it unanimous!" Homer laughed.

We had a wonderful time! Margaret told me that they could be an extra set of grandparents for me. I told her that it would be very nice to have an extra set of grandparents. The white fish was scrumptious as usual! That's because it came fresh right out of Lake Michigan. We drove home and they dropped me off in front of Deck-n-Dock.

"Thank you so much!" I said.

"You're welcome, dear!" They answered.

Just think how lucky I was...two days of birthday celebration!

32 A WEEKEND ON THE "TOM CAT"

It was late August and the days were getting cooler. Uncle Tom was coming up to Hemingway Road and invited Billy and me to spend Saturday and Sunday with him on his cabin cruiser. It was a twenty-four foot "Owens" named The Tom Cat. Uncle Tom would be coming up late that night and spending the night with Grammy at *Little Brown House*. Uncle Tom was always a lot of fun!

"I've packed both warm and cool clothes for you two because you just can't tell what the weather is going to be like," said Mom.

Mom had packed my clothes in a big whale canvass bag the cousins had given to me for my birthday. They had gotten it at a store with cute beach-themed gifts called *Shop of the Gulls*. They also gave me a little wooden sailor man with a mother sailor inside and a baby sailor inside the mother.

Saturday morning came and I saw Uncle Tom walk out of *Little Brown House*. I went running down to him.

"Hi!" Uncle Tom cheerfully said. "Well, if it isn't Alishy the Fishy!" That's what he always called me.

Billy ran down to greet Uncle Tom as well.

"When are we leaving?" Billy asked.

"Well, how about in ten or fifteen minutes?" Uncle Tom asked.

"How can we do that?" Bill asked. "The boat is still at Uncle Jim's marina."

"No, I went into Charlevoix and brought it back here early this morning," said Uncle Tom. "It's tied up over at Margaret and Homer's."

It was a cool, windy day, but the sun was shining. The white caps were in abundance all over the lake.

As we got ready to go, Mom and Dad walked us over to Margaret and Homer's dock to say goodbye.

"Put this coat on, Alicia," said Mom. "It's going to be chilly out on the lake."

We climbed aboard the Tom Cat. Mom and Dad waved goodbye as we backed out and headed out to sea.

"I'll bring them back sometime tomorrow!" Uncle Tom shouted to them.

The Tom Cat's engines were very loud. As we got out into the big part of the lake, we really started to bounce around.

"Do you want to go below into the cabin?" Uncle Tom asked.

"Yes," I replied. "So I can get out of the wind."

It was really neat down in the cabin. There was a little kitchen, a table, and the big bed in the bow. Uncle Tom came down after a while.

"How are you doing, Alishy the Fishy?"

"Just fine!"

"Okay, I'll see you in a while," he said as he went back up.

I laid down on the bow and started to giggle because the waves were really making the bow bounce. I must have fallen asleep because when I went back up, we were coming into a boat harbor.

"Where are we?" I asked.

"We're in Petoskey," answered Uncle Tom.

We tied up in the harbor and went to get dinner. We had the best hamburgers, milk shakes, and French fries I'd ever had!

We walked around Petoskey for a while. I loved a shop called The Mole Hole. It had such cute things in it.

As it grew dark, we went back to the Tom Cat. We sat up on the deck and watched other people on their boats and the stars as they came out.

"Who's up for a game of cards?" Uncle Tom asked.

"I am," said Billy.

"Me too!" I said.

We turned some lights on and played cards until it was time to go to bed. The gentle waves in the harbor rocked us all night long. The next morning, we had cereal for breakfast. Then, we headed back to Hemingway Road. What a fun weekend we had aboard the Tom Cat!

33 HEMINGWAY ROAD RECIPIES

During the winter months in lower Michigan, our menu was different from our summer menu. We went from all sorts of crock pot stews and soups to fabulous summer barbeques and cook-outs! Here are some of the Hein-Shepard favorites! By the way, these recipes are only meant for the "good ole summertime!"

DAD'S LAKE CHARLEVOIX PERCH, SMALL MOUTH BASS, AND ROCK BASS (COOKED BY MOM)

Take each fish fillet and dip it in this mixture:

1 cup flour

1 teaspoon of salt

1 teaspoon of pepper

½ teaspoon of Lawry's salt

Coat each piece well. Heat ¼ cup of oil in electric frying pan. Put in fish and cover. Turn every few minutes for about 15 or 20 minutes.

Serve with:

Blueberry muffins, wild rice and sweet peas

CORN

Shuck some fresh corn on the cob. Have your Mom boil ears of corn in large, covered kettle on the stove. (Though, no corn will be as sweet as Mrs. Hammond's). Spread each ear with butter and salt. Enjoy!

MASHED POTATOES

Take 6 to 8 large potatoes. With Mom's help, wash and peel the potatoes. Cut into sections. Place in 3 quarts of water and boil until cooked. Drain. Add ¾ cup of milk and ¼ cup of butter or margarine. Mix with hand mixer until lumps disappear.

SAUCY DOGS

Great for birthday parties!

2 packages of all-beef hot dogs (diced)

½ cup pickle relish

¼ cup finely chopped onion

2 cups diced American cheese

2 tablespoons Worcestershire sauce

¼ cup mustard

½ cup ketchup

1 can tomato soup

Mix all ingredients in a large bowl. Spoon this mix into hot dog buns. Wrap each bun in tin foil. Put them on a tray in 350 degree oven for 20 minutes. YUMMY!

Serve with:
Jell-O, baked beans, and potato chips.

BARBEQUED CHICKEN (ON DAD'S WEBBER KETTLE)

Split broilers (or whole chickens cut in half). Wash thoroughly. Have Mom or Dad tend to the barbeque. Cook chicken well! Ten minutes before removing from grill, coat each piece with one of these sauces:

Melted butter with lemon juice and a dash of pepper (Melts in your mouth!)

Your favorite brand of barbeque sauce. (Dad always used Open Pit).

BARBEQUED RIBS ON DAD'S WEBBER GRILL

Salt and pepper ribs

Grill ribs until done

Add barbeque sauce. Turn and add sauce to other side.

Serve with:
Grammy's potato salad and biscuits.

GRAMMY'S POTATO SALAD

Boil 8 to 10 large potatoes. Drain water and dice potatoes.

Potato Salad Sauce:

¼ cup minced onion

½ cup mayonnaise

½ cup sour cream

2 tablespoons vinegar

½ cup white sugar

Mix sauce ingredients and stir into diced potatoes. Refrigerate and layer top with sliced hard-boiled eggs.

LAKE CHARLEVOIX FISH FRY

You can use:

Small mouth bass

Rock bass

Perch

Clean and scale fish. Wash fish fillets. Dip into flour with salt and pepper. Melt margarine or butter in fry pan. Put fish in pan on medium to medium high. Turn 3 or 4 times. You can tell the fish are done when it is white and flaky. (Watch out for bones!)

CORNBREAD

Use any cornbread mix and follow package instructions. Serve piping hot!

MRS. HAMMOND'S GREEN BEANS

Wash, snap and cook fresh whole green beans in 2 quarts of salted water until tender.

DAD'S FAMOUS WEBBER KETTLE LONDON BROIL STEAK, OR CHUCK ROAST

Mix together:

1/3 cup soy sauce

1/3 cup vinegar

1½ tablespoons sugar

Dash of ginger

Dash of garlic powder

Sprinkle roast with seasoned salt, poke holes in roast with fork, and pour mixture over roast. Marinate for 4-6 hours. Barbeque 8 to 10 minutes each side.

Serve with:

Mashed potatoes and tossed green salad.

GRAMMY'S EXQUISITE TUNA NOODLE SALAD

1 large can of tuna

1 package large shell pasta, boiled

½ cup chopped celery

¼ cup finely chopped green pepper

¼ teaspoon salt

¼ teaspoon pepper

½ cup mayonnaise

Mix together for the best tuna salad you'll ever taste! Great on a hot day.

Serve with:
Cornbread, warm from the oven with butter.

BISQUICK STRAWBERRY SHORTCAKE

Follow shortcake instructions on Bisquick box. Mash 2 quarts of strawberries with ¾ cup sugar. Slice warm shortcake into pieces. Pour strawberries on top. Top with whipped cream and serve.

See you next summer...

Made in the USA
Middletown, DE
26 May 2020